RESOLVING CONFLICTS IN
ORGANIZATIONS

The Mike Pedler Library

Developing people and organizations

General Editor: Dr Mike Pedler

Books published simultaneously in this series:

Reg Revans
ABC of Action Learning

Nancy M. Dixon
Dialogue at Work

Mike Pedler and Kath Aspinwall
A Concise Guide to the Learning Organization

Rennie Fritchie and Malcolm Leary
Resolving Conflicts in Organizations

Would you like to receive regular information about forthcoming new books in the Mike Pedler Library? Would you like to send us your comments about the book you have read? If so, we would be very pleased to hear from you.

Lemos & Crane
20 Pond Square
Highgate Village
London N6 6BA
England
Tel   +44(0)181 348 8263
Fax   +44(0)181 347 5740
Email admin@lemos.demon.co.uk

Resolving Conflicts in Organizations

DAME RENNIE FRITCHIE DBE AND MALCOLM LEARY

Lemos&Crane

This edition first published in Great Britain 1998
Lemos & Crane
20 Pond Square
Highgate Village
London N6 6BA

© Rennie Fritchie and Malcolm Leary, 1998

ISBN 1-898001-45-6

A CIP catalogue record for this book is available from the British Library.

Designed and typeset by DAP Ltd, London
Printed and bound by Redwood Books, Trowbridge

Contents

INTRODUCTION TO THE LIBRARY

"All learning is for the sake of action, and all action for the sake of friendship." John Macmurray

At the end of centuries and especially millennia, all manner of prophecies break out and gain hold in the public imagination. The world of business and management is no exception to this law as it entertains a great variety of excited ideas for dealing with the better ordering of business and corporate affairs in the face of the supposed end of certainty and, with this, the arts of prediction and strategic planning. In their place we are offered notions of paradox, of chaos and boundlessness, of multiple dilemmas and complexity theory. And these are merely at the "softer" end; at the other there is much old wine in new bottles as the nostrums of Taylorism and Fordism suffuse the apparently novel re-engineering and quality movements.

The value of learning

To be responsive to change, a child, adult, organization, even a society, must be adept at learning. Learning is the means not only of acquiring new knowledge and skill but also of making sense of our lives - individually and collectively - in increasingly fragmented times. We may not know "the how" of this or that, but we can go on hopefully in pursuit of learning a way through. In the absence of a plan, a blueprint for success, we can learn our way forward, growing in confidence as to what we can do and in who we are, making our own path.

For organizations, with an average lifespan of 40 years and declining, learning has become essential for survival

(De Geus). Organizational learning has also been suggested as the only sustainable source of competitive advantage (Senge) and the single most important quality which can be developed and traded (Garratt).

At community or society level new efforts at collaborative action and learning in public forums to tackle the "wicked" problems of poverty, inequality, pollution, crime and public safety look so much more relevant than the old questions of left or right, public or private, electoral democracy or entrepreneurial leadership.

For societies, communities, organizations and individuals the questions are similar: how can we develop those things which we do best so as to be able to trade, exchange, learn, whilst not shutting our eyes to the downsides, shadows, problems and consequences? How can we release energy, potential, self-reliability and active citizenship and build wealth, well-being, collective security, welfare, public services and generally improve the quality of our lives?

A Learning Society?

In an era characterised by large organizations and complexity, it has become plain that individual learning, however impressive, cannot alone resolve problems in relationships - be they at personal, team or organizational level. Equally, it is becoming clear that even the very best of our organizations, private or public, cannot alone resolve the intractable issues of communities and societies. The idea of the "learning organization" is a recognition of, and one response to, the limits of individual learning. But more is needed; there are urgent tasks to hand which go beyond the scope and remit of any single organization or coalition of agencies. As touched on above, these issues demand the organization of action and learning in a different context, and one which is scarcely yet glimpsed, yet alone grasped. In such an ideal collaboration as a Learning Society, there is:

- The freedom to learn - or not to learn - for individuals.

- An organizational aim to support the learning of all members and stakeholders and a desire to transform the organization, as a whole and when appropriate, in creating new products, services and relationships.

- A social drive to provide equality of opportunity for learning to all citizens, at least partly in order that they might contribute to that society being a good place to live in.

The links in this collaborative ideal can be represented diagramatically as follows:

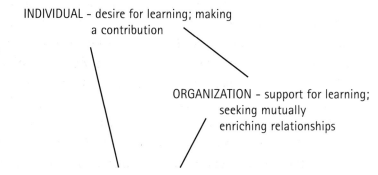

INDIVIDUAL - desire for learning; making a contribution

ORGANIZATION - support for learning; seeking mutually enriching relationships

COMMUNITY/SOCIETY - equal opportunities for learning; providing a good place to live

This manifesto is of course a re-interpretation of old revolutionary aspirations - Liberty (for individuals), the ruling value of Fraternity for organizations, and a duty of Equality of treatment and opportunity in the social sphere.

To each of these we hope to make a contribution, without being confined or encompassed by ideas of personal self-development, or of organizational change, learning, and transformation, nor yet by those of community development or social policy. If a book focuses on, say, organizational processes, then it also keeps an eye on the personal and social development aspects; if it is primarily aimed at the self-development of individuals, then this is in the context of working in organizations and living in society.

The books in the Library are concerned with learning and action on such pressing issues facing us as people working in organizations, living in communities, cities and societies. And whilst there is no single philosophy here, there is an implied criticism of the economic and cultural consensus which underlies much business and management literature in particular. There are challenges here for those who tend to assume that our future rests on the "roll out" of global, information-based capitalism supported by the spread of liberalism and democracy. There is support here for those who question whether individual or organizational development aimed at "high performance" or "excellence" inevitably leads only to desirable outcomes. Here, the irony of the self-proclaimed "learning organization" that is still not a healthy place for people to work in or to live next to, is noted. Here is an aspiration to engage our "best and brightest" and our talent for organizing with some of the really difficult and intractable issues facing us. Above all, we seek to be inclusive and to sustain and support all those trying to learn new things in order to act differently in pursuit of friendship.

Beyond ideas to useful action

Because action and learning require more than just good ideas, the Library is characterised by two more "laws of three". In terms of content, each book contains:

- *educational input* - ideas of substance that you need to know about.

- *invitations to action* - at various points it is suggested that you need to stop and to actually do something with the ideas in order to learn.

- *ethical or political elements* - being an honest colleague, doing the "right thing", seeking good purposes or responding to difficult tasks and circumstances usually imply ethical dilemmas or struggle and perhaps the need for moral support in action and learning.

In terms of pitch or level, though they aim to be attractive and accessible, these books are not "easy reads". Not content with theories and suspicious of easy answers, tools and techniques, these books offer a middle ground of active methods and approaches to the problems and questions posed. Here is an invitation to self-confrontation for the reader. Aware of the complexity and of the questions to which there are no answers, nevertheless there are ways forward, structures to use, directions to follow in order to engage your own energies, the ingenuity of colleagues and the aspirations of customers or those you serve in order to learn your way through. You can't put such a book down without at least thinking of doing something differently.

MIKE PEDLER

FOREWORD

It is very good to welcome Rennie Fritchie and Malcolm Leary to this series. Both of them are colleagues of many years' standing whose work has attained a particular prominence in the field of handling conflict.

The significance of their work is in addressing the tough issue of conflict in a field of practice – organizational development and human resources management – where many practitioners choose to take an optimistic, humanistic stance. Much of the writing on learning organizations for example, is characterised by underlying assumptions that, "all will be for the best in this best of all possible worlds". Yet as Richard Pascale has pointed out in his excellent *Managing on the Edge* the learning organization is likely to see more rather than less conflict as diversity is encouraged and different views compete for attention and resources.

In *Resolving Conflicts in Organizations* Rennie and Malcolm show a constructive way to recognise and deal with this "shadow side" to development, change and growth. Lively organizations create plenty of spaces for disagreements, and the skilful handling of these prevents the escalation of healthy difference into bitter feuding whilst creating confidence in people that they can contend and collaborate. The insightful models of conflict and the activities offered here for resolving them will give all pioneers and innovators fresh heart.

MIKE PEDLER

Dedicated to Dr Fritz Glasl whose early work on conflict developed the models, and whose continued work deepens the thinking and learning.

1 Introduction

There is conflict in all organizations. Some conflicts are inconsequential. Others are disruptive and painful for those involved, but have little impact on those around them. Some people use conflict for their own ends as part of an elaborate game of office politics. So they do not want a resolution. The conflict is serving their purposes. Conflict can also be used by some as an unappealing way of demonstrating authority. They too do not want to change.

Whether or not people want to resolve them, conflicts affect morale, communication and productivity. The price of conflict is paid by organizations, employers, colleagues as well as by protagonists. At the most serious levels conflicts can bring teams, departments and sometimes whole organizations to a virtual standstill.

Although conflicts are everywhere present, and there is not always a joint will to resolve them, they are neither inevitable, insoluble nor unmanageable. Nor is it the case that conflicts can only be resolved by "natural healers", people with the personality of a conflict resolver. Resolving conflict requires tools, approaches, understanding and the capacity for insight and learning. With this in mind more and more people are seeking to acquire the skills and behaviour of conflict resolution, in order that they can help themselves and others to deal with everyday life at work.

When conflicts "erupt" in an organization a first reaction is often to look for someone to blame. If no one is readily available people may be left feeling that they are suffering from an unpleasant infection, struggling to come to terms with the resulting discomfort and disruption. People can understand conflicts at an intellectual level, but emotions can leave them feeling powerless and perplexed.

Much more can be done to prevent and resolve the conflicts in organizational life. The twin emphases in this book are on first learning what to do, and then doing it and learning from the experience. In this way, responses to conflict can be improved each time they occur.

WHY PEOPLE NEED TO RESOLVE CONFLICT

Here are some typical reasons managers have given for wanting to improve their responses to conflict and their ability to resolve it.

> "My director is driving me crazy!"
>
> "I manage people who take risks."
>
> "Do I learn to live with conflict or do something about it?"
>
> "I need to learn to say 'No'."
>
> "I have difficulty in letting go of a conflict."
>
> "I tend to withdraw when dealing with aggression in colleagues and I am not happy about this."
>
> "The workplace is full of conflict and I seem to get drawn in."
>
> "Conflict is much more open today. It seems to be built in to how we work"
>
> "I need help to deal with petty squabbles."
>
> "I need help with the inter-personal issues at the moment; anything I do seems to make it worse."

"I need help in resolving other people's conflicts."

"Conflict handling is an essential skill in today's world and I need to improve my skills."

"I need to understand the causes of external conflicts."

"I want to know what the drivers of conflict and change are."

"We are losing good people who leave when the conflict gets out of hand."

Over 80 per cent of more than 500 managers we have worked with reported conflicts that had escalated to serious levels – where the situation gets "out of hand" and people choose to leave their organization.

Why are conflicts so difficult to resolve? Conflict can bring out the worst in people, particularly at work where rational, adult behaviour is the norm. In a conflict the opposite is common. People become so emotional and irrational that they cannot be objective about the original problem. Individuals form into groups unified against a perceived enemy. A group in conflict soon develops an identity and a life of its own, which becomes more intense in its wish to defeat the "other side".

UNDERLYING PRINCIPLES OF CONFLICT RESOLUTION

The beliefs underlying our approach to resolving conflicts in organizations are summarised in the following list and subsequently developed in the book.

- You can learn important lessons from understanding and working with your conflicts.
- Development can start with a conflict only if we can learn enough from it.

- Conflicts are part of the human condition and organizational life.
- Action is needed to resolve conflicts: they do not cure themselves.
- Action to resolve conflicts must be based on an understanding of the forces that are driving it, otherwise you could make it worse.
- Choose your action/intervention carefully: look at all the options.
- Action should be based on principles which you have worked out for yourself.
- Maintain your integrity at all times and protect yourself, otherwise you will be of no use to anyone.
- Good intentions are not enough: they are necessary, but not sufficient in themselves.
- Sensitive, timely and skilled intervention is needed, appropriate to the circumstances of the conflict.
- You may not be able to do everything yourself. So others from within your organization or outside may needed if a particular expertise, skill or role is required.

RESOLVING CONFLICT IN THE SUBJECTIVE SPHERE

Traditional methods of conflict resolution focus on the objective sphere without paying due regard to the subjective element – the attitudes, feelings, perceptions and behaviour of the people involved. All problems underlying the conflict are believed to have a logical, rational solution. But subjective distortions and damage caused by intense personal involvement make rational discussion difficult if not impossible. Conflicts are more than disputes with logical solutions to be uncovered.

It is little use tackling the objective sphere first in all but the most minor of conflicts. The conflict may have begun with an objective issue, but all the subjective distortions and damage have also to be dealt with; only then will the parties be in a position to start to address the objective difficulties.

Many approaches are tried in the search for logical solutions to objective problems, for example:

Make the system work

Here it is assumed that a system's implementation causes the conflict, not the system itself. Sometimes this is true; many conflicts do arise out of badly implemented systems but a fundamental weakness in the system may also be contributing. When problems continue it is assumed they will be solved by putting the system into practice more resolutely.

Set up additional machinery

A person is appointed or a body is set up to police relationships between the parties or act as the co-ordinating function. A complete separation may have arisen between the parties trying to work out an agreement and those responsible for implementing that agreement. This often happens when those responsible for reaching an agreement will not have the task of implementing it.

Changing the organizational structure

Changes are made to the technical interpretation of the problem. Organization structures are altered accordingly. New procedures allocate new responsibilities, align new functions and relationships and control the operation of the system. Structural changes increase constraints and controls as a way of squeezing out conflict. Structures can also be loosened to allow people to have more responsibility and increase their capacity to "sort things out for themselves".

In many cases the net result of these objective strategies is to further escalate an existing conflict, because they fail to address underlying issues of temperament, group dynamics, relationships and emotions.

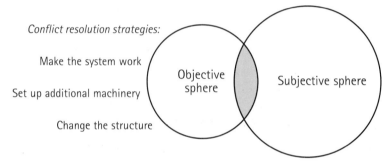

It is essential to begin in the subjective sphere when resolving a conflict. To attempt to get everyone round a table to discuss the problem and resolve it hardly ever works, because feelings and behaviours get in the way. Forced agreement and solutions are later subverted and sabotaged. The conflict is then ready to escalate. The procedure outlined below for your conflict resolution can be interpreted in diagrammatic form as follows:

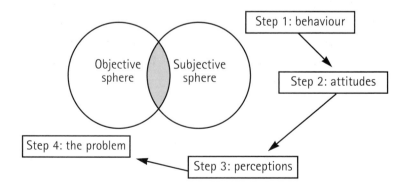

Subjective sphere strategies

Even when the subjective sphere influences are taken into account, conflict resolution strategies may not work because they only affect one element of a complex interplay. Three elements make up the subjective sphere of a conflict: behaviour, attitudes and perceptions. Resolution strategies which aim to put right the difficulties in one area, whilst ignoring the other two will not work in the longer term.

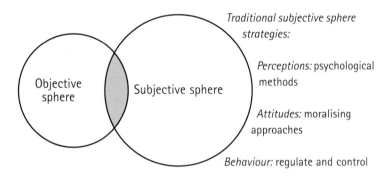

Traditional subjective sphere strategies:

Perceptions: psychological methods

Attitudes: moralising approaches

Behaviour: regulate and control

Objective sphere

Subjective sphere

Resolving conflicts involves understanding individuals and the groups that are formed when conflict takes shape; evaluating what approach is best to deal with the parties in conflict; and acting out this strategy, remaining aware of the dynamics involved and how different approaches are needed at different stages of conflict. It is assumed throughout the book that parties in conflict carry equal importance in the organization so that domination over one by another does not occur through use of an inherent power structure (see Chapter 5).

LEARNING FROM CONFLICT

The impact of conflict is invariably negative. Conflict can undermine or destroy people's self-confidence and self-esteem. It can also damage the effectiveness of teams, departments and indeed whole organizations. But, as we have said, conflicts are an opportunity to learn – to see other people's perceptions of your behaviour, to witness group dynamics at work and show the destructive consequence of aggressive, passive or manipulative behaviour.

We would go further to say not only can people learn from conflict, but in order successfully to resolve a conflict people *must* learn. They must learn how to influence other people's attitudes, perceptions and behaviour. More important than that, to create a win-win resolution, the protagonists are *all* going to have to learn new attitudes, perceptions and behaviour. Therein lies the possible positive impact of conflict. If changes to attitudes, perceptions and behaviour are lasting, embedded and internalised – and the need for change is accepted by both sides – development can occur.

With this in mind, we believe that no conflict can be fully resolved by temporary compromises often imposed by third parties and grudgingly accepted by participants. A lasting resolution requires a developmental approach to resolving conflict. This is an approach which allows every one involved to work within a clear analytical framework, with identified roles and skills and appropriate behaviour. Through these structural methods people can learn about themselves and others and develop and change as they resolve the conflict. A less holistic, structural and supportive approach will only produce ephemeral and superficial change.

It is not just individuals that can learn and develop through resolving conflicts. Groups, teams, departments and organizations can too. The need constantly to seek new and better ways of working in all sectors and organizations is widely accepted. New behaviours, processes and approaches devised in the first instance to resolve conflict will only last and spread if they offer functional benefits for everyone. So seeking win-win resolutions that last will contribute to the whole organization changing, developing and approaching being a genuinely learning organization.

THE STRUCTURE OF THE BOOK

In what is to follow we look at the nature of conflict, how it can be classified as "hot" or "cold" (Chapter 2). In Chapter 3 we look at ways of understanding basic human temperaments, how people think, feel and act according to recognisable traits. As individuals form themselves into groups in conflict we see how these groups are overtaken by a dynamism that causes the conflict to worsen – Chapter 4 describes this process. Conflict escalates systematically through various levels, from discussion to destruction – the Conflict Escalator, which expresses these changes figuratively, is presented in Chapter 5. Chapters 6, 7, 8 and 9 look at means of resolving conflict. Based on the earlier framework, approaches, skills and techniques are presented that will enable managers to approach their particular conflict empowered with suitable developmental strategies. These will involve where possible the protagonists themselves instigating and activating conflict resolution, though third party expertise may at some extreme stages be needed.

The Appendix contains discussions of other psychological models to contribute to an overall understanding of human behaviour, particularly in the context of conflict. These are designed to deepen and enrich the reader's insight, enhancing but not replacing the structured approach set out in the main text.

HOW TO USE THIS BOOK

To get the most out of this book you will need to draw on an example of conflict from your own experience. This will form what we call "your living case study". Throughout the book this is a reference point and testing ground for ways of looking at and resolving conflict that will work for you. The best opportunities for learning are provided by current circumstances in which you are involved or can observe. Alternatively, you can use a past conflict that still concerns and puzzles you. There are 10 Activities throughout the book to assist you in developing your own case study. To gain the most from these Activities, carry them out as you are reading the book. They are designed to be tools to assist understanding and reflection, to help you prepare your own responses and approaches to the conflict. The first Activity follows on the next page. It is a key building block in using the book and should be considered before proceeding to Chapter 2. The other Activities are collected at the back of the book (from page 135 onwards) to avoid interrupting the flow of the text. A button arrow in the text marks each Activity and on which page it can be found.

Activity 1: Basic Questionnaire

Think about the conflict you have identified as your living case study and answer the following questions about it. At this stage do not think too deeply about the situation; you will be able to analyse things more later on, using various devices designed for the purpose. At this stage put down your first impressions and your immediate thoughts.

1. How would you describe the conflict? Can you give it a name or a simple description?

2. What did the conflict appear to be about when it started?

3. Over time did the reasons for the conflict shift or change?

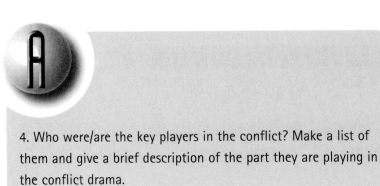

4. Who were/are the key players in the conflict? Make a list of them and give a brief description of the part they are playing in the conflict drama.

5. Give examples of typical incidents or behaviour.

Example 1

Example 2

Example 3

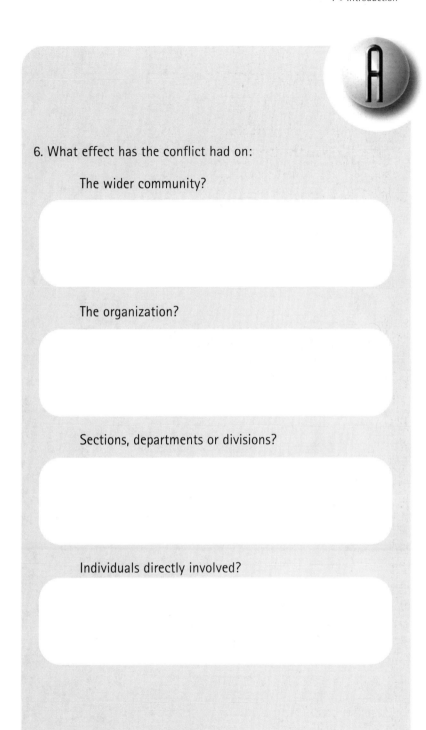

6. What effect has the conflict had on:

The wider community?

The organization?

Sections, departments or divisions?

Individuals directly involved?

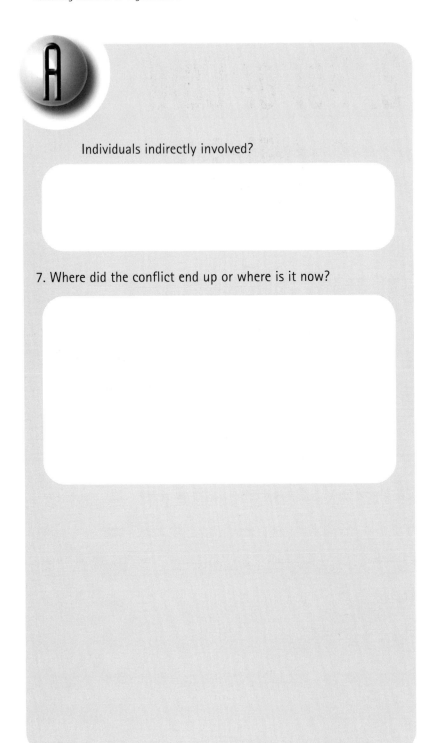

Individuals indirectly involved?

7. Where did the conflict end up or where is it now?

2. Hot or Cold Conflict

IN THIS CHAPTER: *The nature of conflict: how it can be classified as hot or cold.*

Contents

2 Hot or Cold Conflict

The most easily identifiable feature of conflicts is the degree, intensity, or "temperature" of the behaviour involved. Is the conflict hot or cold? This notion will be used – as we show in later chapters – to point towards the kind of action that is appropriate in resolving a particular conflict. Hot and cold conflict is one of the seminal models and frameworks developed by Professor Fritz Glasl on which our work is founded. A detailed description of the theoretical basis to conflict resolution is given in Professor Glasl's paper to the Congress on Conflict Management entitled "The Process of Escalation of Conflict" (NPI, Holland, 1980).

CHARACTERISTICS OF HOT CONFLICT

An irritation that burrowed, to
A reaction which was heated, to
An exchange which was angry, to
A skirmish which expanded, to
A fury which erupted, to
A tumult of larger numbers, to
A frantic exchange of data, to
A growing band of warriors, to

Battles which were counted, to
Ideals loudly spouted, to
Humiliations which were heaped, to
Explosions which were noisy, to
Engagements which were bloody, to
Outright war which was pointless, to
Casualties which were endless, from
An irritation that burrowed.

RENNIE FRITCHIE

You can't miss hot conflict. As the temperature rises, apparently erratic or aggressive behaviour and strong words become more common. Hot conflicts often involve intense personal confrontation. The following report gives the flavour of a hot conflict between the two senior managers of a major art establishment.

> *"Last week in front of a number of staff the row between the Secretary and the Director reached a deafening crescendo with the two adversaries allegedly coming to blows. Explaining the vitriolic slanging match the Director said, 'We work together and occasionally things can get a little heated. She (the Secretary) is unbelievably talented and sometimes such people can be difficult'."*

The degree reached by hostilities will be "hot" if some or all of the following characteristics are apparent.

High ideals and high self-esteem

People feel strongly about the higher motives for their actions and feel good about their involvement, even if they know that the impact on others may be painful or detrimental.

Enthusiasm to achieve particular goals

People are highly energetic in fighting to win each "battle" in a "war". They set goals and achieve them to score points off others along the way.

Blindness about motives/illusions of clarity

When asked people can give clear answers about why they are involved in a conflict, for example, "for the good of the service", "for the principles of the profession", "to maintain our position". However, whilst these may have been the prompts to get involved initially, motives often degenerate, for instance, "to teach them a lesson", "to see them squirm", "to put them in their place", "to eliminate them". As long as more positive reasons for involvement can be offered the darker motivation often remains unseen.

Hectic activity

Activity in the conflict becomes hectic, with many skirmishes. Misunderstandings arise from misinformation, posturing, meetings (or meetings about meetings), and plotting and scheming. The effect is like a disturbed hornets' nest.

Explosions

Hot conflicts are peppered with explosions, both big and small. People lose their tempers. There are angry incidents and unseemly outbursts. Temper tantrums and critical incidents are frequent and are often exaggerated in the re-telling.

Sensitivity

During a hot conflict people are extra sensitive. An unintended action may be interpreted as a deliberate slight. For example, "Did you see how everyone else's name was in alphabetical order on the memo but I was added on at the end?", "They called everyone by their first name except me", and "Did you see how my question was ignored?".

Engagement

In a hot conflict people forcefully and deliberately search each other out. They go to meetings they would otherwise avoid just to have the opportunity of a confrontation. They take lunch at particular times or in particular places to increase the chances of "bumping into" the enemy.

Information overload

Rumours abound. Information and misinformation flows freely. Any data is welcomed. Little care is taken to verify it. The whispering campaign is conducted in a sophisticated and instrumental way. Unchecked gossip leads to sensationalising.

Charged atmosphere

A charged atmosphere can quickly overheat. People are alert and ready at all times with occasional bouts of exhaustion in between.

CHARACTERISTICS OF COLD CONFLICT

> An irritation that burrowed, to
> Withdrawal that was calculated, to
> Distance which was palpable, to
> Rules which were unspoken, to
> Silence which was deafening, to
> Accommodation which was hidden, to
> Rejection of all interest, to
> Guilt which was shameful, to
> Denial that was vehement, to
> Ignoring that was hurtful, to
> A cold shoulder that was obvious, to
> An atmosphere which was chilling, to
> Hypothermia of emotions, to
> A numbing that was blunting, to
> A shutdown that was fatal, from
> An irritation that burrowed.
>
> RENNIE FRITCHIE

Cold conflicts are much less likely to be evident to a newcomer. Indeed it is possible to work with colleagues engaged in cold conflict for some months before becoming aware of the hostility and its full extent. An example of cold conflict involved a group of college lecturers in pursuit of a wage claim. To the amusement of their colleagues, they threatened the college authorities that if their demands were not met in full they would have recourse to the "withdrawal of their enthusiasm", the existence of "enthusiasm" having been scarcely apparent hitherto. Where parties are conducting a cold conflict, some or all of the following characteristics are discernible.

Cynicism about ideals and low self-esteem

People feel cynical about any higher purpose for the conflict and are dismissive and sarcastic about those involved, sometimes including themselves. They rarely discuss, or publicly engage in, the conflict. They are evidently not proud of their actions on the rare occasions they do.

Goals are absent

Energy levels are low in a cold conflict. There is no particular desire to win battles or score points. Cold conflict is more a long-term war of attrition than an intense battle campaign.

Blindness about effects of own behaviour on others

In a longer-term cold conflict the climate can be permanently cool with seasons of frosty hostility. People can work in the same room or building for years in near silent animosity. Light, space, air and spontaneity find it difficult to enter. An icy calm descends. Those who set the temperature interpret the absence of cross words as a sign that no one is adversely affected. This hypothermic atmosphere can slow energy so that the conflict reaches an impasse and a feeling of inevitability can take hold.

Distance between parties

Those involved become distant – little or no communication, no messages, meetings or information. The parties stand on either side of a great yawning chasm facing in opposite directions. A lack of interest in the situation and the other party is the order of the day.

Implosions

Cold conflicts have few outward signs. Instead of explosive incidents occasional implosions occur where people stoically absorb strong feelings and collapse inwardly, leaving dark and empty emotional spaces.

Insensitivity

People toughen up outwardly so that they seem impervious to hurt and slights. Or they seek to appear so. Even the most direct attack seems to slide off their Teflon-coated skin. Verbal assaults are ignored, and when pressed those involved use expressions like, "I've got better things to do than worry about them".

Avoidance

Highly sophisticated means of avoidance are developed. For example, if one person attends a meeting, the other will be absent. If they have to attend the same function they keep on the move and never come face to face. It seems almost choreographed. Over time these unspoken methods can develop into rigid rules where people talk through third parties even though the other person is there.

Information starvation

Few rumours circulate as there is little happening to talk about. Information is not invited, not welcomed and certainly not shared.

Freezing

Cold conflicts are nearly always frozen and stuck with an air of immovability and intractability. Things seem impossible to grasp hold of and the chilled atmosphere can slowly disable onlookers and bystanders. Senses are dulled; the whole procedure is exhausting.

To assess the temperature of your conflict, turn to:

ACTIVITY 2 Page 141

3. Personal Preferences and Characteristics

IN THIS CHAPTER: Ways of understanding basic human temperament: how people think, feel and act according to recognisable traits.

Contents

3 Personal Preferences and Characteristics

PREFERENCES FOR HOT OR COLD METHODS

Personality, professional background or occupation may push us towards preferring a hot or cold conflict. For example, some work is associated with risk-taking, extrovert behaviour and volatility, all of which are symptoms of hot conflict. Cold conflict is most likely where the occupation requires a more calculated, measured, rational approach. Management styles also influence the temperature of a conflict. There may be an emphasis on "hot" – where more risky, confrontational, intuitive, challenging behaviour is encouraged – or "cold" where logic, rationality and calculation is the order of the day.

To evaluate your own personal preferences for hot or cold methods in conflicts turn now to:

ACTIVITY 3 Page 146

TEMPERAMENTS

In everyday use the term "temperament" describes a person's character as determined by their physical or emotional constitution, which permanently affects their behaviour (such as "nervous temperament" or "artistic temperament"). The term also has a more particular use in folklore, drama, and literature. It describes well-recognised clusters of broadly connected behaviour, feeling and thinking. Traditionally there are four temperaments – choleric, melancholic, phlegmatic and sanguine. As a management tool, these temperaments are discussed by Dr Tom Boydell in *Management Self-Development* (ILO Management Series No.21, Geneva, 1985). There are of course other methods of exploring or typologising different ways of seeing people and interpreting their behaviour in a conflict. These include the paradigms of Parent-Adult-Child and Victim-Persecutor-Rescuer, which are outlined in the Appendix. However we find in the context of conflicts that the use of the temperaments is the most helpful.

The following describes the characteristics associated with each temperament and how they react to conflict. Individual temperament indicates likely choices and preferences in what you think, feel and behave. The way you think creates your views on life, your ideas and opinions, your ideals, how you present information and thoughts to others and how you prefer others' information and thoughts to be presented to you. Further, your temperament influences your aspirations, drives and motives and how these are expressed. Reaction to other people, events and circumstances arise from deep-seated motivations and preferences. Because temperament is such a powerful factor in daily interactions, it becomes more pronounced when differences create conflict.

At the end of this Chapter we invite you to reflect on your main and associated or "back-up" temperament. The back-up temperament will act to moderate anything someone does and support the best efforts that result from the main temperament.

Choleric

Some people are described as "fiery". Powerfulness, strong will and initiative are common characteristics. They enjoy challenges and apply their energies wholeheartedly to whatever they decide to do. They have an independent outlook and display leadership qualities. They stand out in a crowd. What they do is highly visible. They may be known for being something of a visionary, looking to the future, often seeing things with intuition and instinct. They step in "where angels fear to tread", show courage and take risks when others might hold back. They have strong opinions, inner convictions, certain beliefs and motives and can draw other people in with their enthusiasm and determination.

They can get emotional – often out of a sense of righteous indignation and anger. They can be highly judgmental and impetuous. Things can be forced through at the expense of others' feelings with an adverse effect on friendships and other relationships. Their lives are run by a punishing regime with no room for laggards or sitting on the fence. They can be rude and domineering, take too much on themselves and be reluctant to delegate. Lots of hectic activity takes place in their lives – plenty of noise and energy. Sometimes this gets out of control and spills over into disagreements and disputes. At the very worst they become destructive, despairing and violent.

The choleric temperament will prefer a hot conflict. On the other hand a thoroughly cold conflict, featuring avoidance, hiding and distance, would be anathema. Their preferred way of dealing with conflict is to attempt to force people to adopt their way of thinking; take the lead in deciding what needs to be done; and to refuse to recognise any opposition.

Melancholic

Melancholics are down-to-earth with a strong sense of the material and the physical: the basic things of life. They are good at forming and holding things together, being the anchor or at the core of all activities. They are careful and analytical, industrious, methodical and self-disciplined. They are prepared to make personal sacrifices to reach their goals and expect others to be prepared to do the same.

Melancholics make vital contributions in focused and limited areas. They are gifted in what they do, often in a concentrated and ascetic way. They turn the spotlight on themselves, their feelings and responses. They need time to absorb what is going on, to reflect and reach important conclusions for themselves and others.

They rely on their own experiences and observations. They must be convinced with their own eyes. They will probe, question and explore until they are fully satisfied. They will question their own and other people's motives until they are absolutely certain of what is being done and why. They are sometimes perceived as too pedantic and stuck. They have a tendency to be moody, over-critical and over-sensitive, seeing the world in tragic terms with themselves in the middle of it. As a result, they can be hyper-sensitive, unsociable, negative and prejudiced, out of touch with what is really going on and wrapped up in their own world. At worst they become paranoid and hysterical.

Melancholics can be overwhelmed by negativity. Their sensitive, observing nature allows them to see the implications and consequences of a cold conflict clearly. Hot conflicts are unlikely to fit in with the deeper, more considered approach to life which melancholics thrive on. They will seek to gain legitimacy for their point of view and for their ways of thinking in a conflict by example, and try to gain recognition and respect for their ways of doing things.

Phlegmatic

Phlegmatics are most comfortable when they are calm and tranquil. They are known for their dependability, loyalty and understanding. Reliable in habits, they pay attention to analysis and detail. They tend to step back from situations rather than "dive in" and as a consequence their approach is objective and diplomatic.

Phlegmatics like their lives to be ordered and efficiently run. They also bring these qualities into all situations. They are respected for being well organized, efficient and practical. They like relationships to be calm and well ordered too. They use their best efforts to smooth out difficulties. As a result, phlegmatics are easy to get along with, in the main, but difficult to get to know and "read". They are careful in their use of energy and effort. Once things are organized they prefer to stick to the plan and follow the rules. There has to be a good reason for changing things.

If phlegmatics do not get the conditions they prefer or if something disturbs them, they can become resolutely unmotivated – something that takes a long time to rectify. They can procrastinate, be selfish, self-centred and over-protective. Holding back can turn into indecision, worrying and fearfulness.

The phlegmatic temperament will react very badly to the noise, upset and confrontation associated with hot conflict. They will undoubtedly prefer the more measured, careful and cautious, insidious, tactical, political and protective style of a cold conflict – even if the effects are negative in the end. They seek to persuade others to accept their way of thinking as the correct one, a viewpoint to be seriously considered and accepted. The phlegmatic is unlikely to see the negative side, concentrating wholly on what effect the cold conflict is having on them personally.

Sanguine

Sanguine temperaments bring qualities of lightness, levity, spaciousness and movement. Others experience them as always being on the move; busy people who always have somewhere to go, someone to see, something to do. They are outgoing, responsive, warm and friendly, talkative and convivial, enjoying their own and other people's company. They are rarely boring, are interested and enthusiastic, keen to involve themselves in other people's issues and problems and to do something about them. They also want other people to participate and be involved.

In contrast they also live strongly in their own inner world, which is full of moving pictures, possibilities, options and prospects. They are keen observers, are acutely aware of what is happening, how people are, who is saying what to whom and so on. Sanguines are attracted to people and situations and once they are "there" they like to feel accepted and wanted, for themselves and their contribution. Their responses are varied and they like to move quickly from one situation to another. They are generally optimistic about the future, but they can get restless in their desire to get on with things.

They may have a reputation for being a bit unreliable, undisciplined and "all over the place", forgetful and dismissive. It may be a case of "out of sight, out of mind" and they may make promises that are not kept. Sometimes they do go "over the top" and can be prone to exaggeration and over-emphasis. At the very worst, they become hysterical.

The sanguine temperament will probably interpret a cold conflict in the worst possible light. The lack of direct evidence that something is going on, but the overwhelming feeling that bad things are happening and being done to them, could turn a sanguine person paranoid. All the latent fears, insecurities and hyper-sensitivities of the sanguine are irritated by a cold conflict. Their preferred way of dealing with conflict is to bring others round to their way of thinking in whatever ways they can, and behave expediently as they see fit at the time.

To see how your temperament is affecting your living case study conflict, turn now to the Temperaments Questionnaire in:

ACTIVITY 4 Page 151

4. The Dynamics of Conflict

IN THIS CHAPTER: How groups are formed in conflict, and how these groups can be characterised.

Contents

4 The Dynamics of Conflict

So far we have looked at how conflicts can be broadly categorised as hot or cold, and at the characteristics – temperaments – of individuals. And as we have shown, individuals have preferences for different types of conflict depending on their temperaments. As conflict develops, however, dynamic forces come into operation that escalate the situation such that personal identity diminishes. The demands of conflict create a strongly defined group dynamic. Social complexity grows as the conflict escalates. Parties to the conflict are not content to fight their battles in private. As the conflict grows, each party seeks to encourage, and sometimes force, others to support their cause. Alliances and coalitions are built up. A conflict can move far beyond its original causes and protagonists. The definition of issues at stake becomes a part of what is being contested. When this situation is reached patterns of behaviour, thinking and attitude come into operation, which escalate and worsen the conflict.

UNITY IN ADVERSITY

Parties in conflict have a feeling of togetherness that affects the behaviour and self-image of everyone in the group – whether departments, functions, professions or teams. They think they have common goals or interests. Benignly expressed, it is an "all hands on deck" attitude; when a recognised foe takes shape on the horizon, shoulders are squared and conflict ensues.

FORMATION OF A COHESIVE GROUP

When a group is united in the face of an "enemy", everyone within the group has to be seen to be thinking, feeling and acting together. The more it sees its cause, aims and proposals as right, the more everyone else must be wrong. This feeling of "rightness" and worthiness raises the group's self-esteem – talk of a good team spirit and high group morale is often based on a distorted and overblown self-image. To reinforce this solidarity, self-esteem and feeling of superiority, social bonding and relationships become important. So more socializing, inside and outside work, takes place. Telephone conversations out of work hours increase. Emblems, signs or uniforms are adopted to differentiate from others and as symbols of affiliation to a particular group. The use of technical jargon or specialist language increases, reinforcing the inclusivity of the group and showing others outside the group that they are "excluded". In-jokes become ever more obscure.

CONFORMITY

Sub-groups and cliques disappear, and minorities that may have different opinions or proposals have to adapt themselves quickly to the majority – or else they will find themselves accused of heresy. They may then be thrown out of the group. Differences with people outside the group are seen as threats; differences inside the group are seen as weaknesses. Certain kinds of behaviour and expressions of opinion are declared taboo. These rules cannot be questioned or countered. Conformity reduces or even removes self-doubt or criticism.

THE EMERGENCE OF A LEADER – AND SUBSERVIENT FOLLOWERS

Every group in a conflict needs a strong leader and followers. If the group already has a hierarchical structure this becomes more pronounced, especially in conflicts between different departments. The head of the department exerts ever more rigid censorship in order to protect confidential information, prevent leaks and avoid revealing secrets. All of these might otherwise lead to a weakening of the group's position. The "leader" can therefore behave in a more autocratic way, taking on "emergency powers", "cutting corners". Everyone in the group knows and accepts their place. It is essential to know where everyone is and what they are doing – all the time.

Those with a tendency to be more aggressive, self-confident, willing to take initiatives and act as pioneers – often those with choleric temperaments – come to the fore and find a significant role in the conflict, particularly in hot conflicts. They identify themselves completely with the group on whose behalf they act. The rest of the group – those who are temperamentally less suited to up-front, adversarial action – see their leaders as courageous, steadfast and decisive. These are the qualities and virtues apparently needed to lead the unified group against the enemy.

FURTHER CHARACTERISTICS OF A GROUP IN CONFLICT

Rigidity

Rigidity is common in conflict. Thinking evolves and becomes fixed into set patterns. Views are seen as good or bad. Responses are given as a resounding "Yes" or "No". Feelings that muddy the clear waters of the group's views are unwelcome. The group's views become channelled and restricted. Alternatives, choices and options are not given consideration – it's win or lose.

Distortion

In a conflict perceptions are impaired and information is distorted. Adversarial groups continually judge and misjudge almost everything that is said and done. The overall perception is influenced by selecting, filtering and perverting, turning things into their opposite.

Distorted perceptions have many harmful effects. For example, one party is only interested in seeing the negative in the other. Unfavourable characteristics possessed by "them" (which "we" do not think we possess "ourselves") strike "us" with particular force. Other professions are characterised as "bureaucratic", "insensitive", "rigid", "profit centred", "soft" or "hard", "untidy", "careless" or "lazy". The rift between the parties to the conflict grows greater still, for each knows how it is being thought of, described and labelled. Each party attributes qualities to others, whether or not there is any justification for doing so. It points out dangers that don't exist and sees threats where there are none.

Once a negative image has been built up it must be actively reinforced. Only certain kinds of information that fit into the picture painted get through. Each only sees things that fit the image; or the information is bent, changed and distorted to reinforce the picture each party has already formed.

Stereotyping

All the good characteristics are given to one's own party, all the bad qualities one can think of (and some one can't) are ascribed to the other side. Each group is clearly more intelligent, more humane, cleaner and tidier, more efficient and just made up of better people than the others.

Stereotyping of individuals, groups, teams, professions and functions is part of organization culture. This may be done in a harmless way in normal circumstances, but in a conflict the exchange of prejudice and stereotypes becomes a vicious game. Pejorative labels are used which are then associated with negative qualities and descriptions of typical behaviour, for example: "They will do anything to get their own way" or "They use every trick in the book."

Perversely the very qualities a party admires in itself are then turned around to describe others in derogatory terms. So, "our" courage becomes someone else's recklessness; "our" initiative becomes the other's aggression; "our" flexibility becomes "their" indecisiveness; and "our" steadiness becomes "their" rigidity. Each party values its own "precision" and "carefulness"; in its adversaries it does not like their pedantry.

The forming of stereotypes is then reinforced by projecting this image onto the past ("And as a matter of fact they have always been like that but we have been very tolerant") and foreseeing the future ("And we expect they will always be like this").

Polarisation

The phenomena and symptoms described so far occur because each party can only see any event or person in the conflict from its own perspective. The longer the conflict goes on, the greater the separation of the parties and the more difficult it is to bridge this continually growing gap.

For example, one group or individual thinks they are fully aware of their own motives but cannot comprehend what the motives of the other party might be. After a while the person or group simplifies the thinking and motivation of the other party into crude and blatant caricatures. Later on they don't even think about it.

Nor do they think too much about the effect of their behaviour on the other side. They have little or no idea of the effects their behaviour can have on them. They certainly do not ask them. The others are such remote figures, emotionally if not physically, that one side could not put itself in the other's place even if it wanted to.

They become increasingly irritated and annoyed by the slightest fault or mistake shown by the other side. Conversely, they are amazed that the other side does not appreciate their superiority. It is somehow acceptable for one party to judge others by their actions. When it comes to "us", we should be judged by our intentions.

Little wonder that communication becomes difficult.

Attempts to make contact become increasingly problematical. They cannot meet and reach each other. Deliberately blurring and confusing the other party's intentions makes it impossible to do anything but disapprove of the other's perceived intentions. A party cannot hope to approach others openly if it has disregarded the negative effects of its own behaviour.

Fixing

As the distance between the conflicting parties becomes greater little connection remains. All bridges of positive contact have been burnt as a result of the conflict. Yet psychologically this distance allows each party to treat the others in a way which suspends the ordinary rules of polite behaviour, and brings into play behaviour that would normally be condemned as unfair, inhuman and unjustified. Eventually, the other party is seen as scarcely human. Any possibility of change or development for them is denied. They are judged only by what they have said and done in the past.

Each party therefore comes to the conclusion that "We are only interested in this aim and nothing else". Now that it is clear that the rest of the problem has been identified as belonging to the other group, life becomes much simpler. The parties can test their strengths and weaknesses and try to attack the other side at their most vulnerable spot. Yet at the same time considerations of esteem dominate the situation. Both parties have already manoeuvred themselves into a position where they must show no weakness.

Each party tries to make sure all future events and circumstances will be designed and engineered so that they will not have to change their negative views. Both parties fix each other in the past, trap each other in the present and condemn each other in the future. Any juicy bit of information, any scurrilous piece of gossip, any irrelevant rumour about the other party is saved up so that it can be used at an appropriate moment in the future to do most damage.

5. The Conflict Escalator

IN THIS CHAPTER: How conflict escalates systematically through various levels, from discussion to destruction.

Contents

5 The Conflict Escalator

They disagreed, he said one thing,
she another, hot words, different views,
But they discussed.

By morning stances were taken,
sides chosen, positions marked out.
They debated.

Frustrated by the lack of movement,
he acted just to show her. She reacted only worse.
Deeds not words.

She now saw him as wholly selfish,
he thought she was hard and unforgiving -
Fixed images.

Others saw and were concerned
but she couldn't be seen to give way
and he couldn't be seen to give in -
Loss of face.

The attacks were on, he aggressive, threatening,
She, undaunted, upping the ante, laying down trip-wires -
Strategies of threat.

He's a beast and he deserves what he gets,
She's a monster from the female regiment,
the ends now justify the means.
Inhuman.

He's prevented from going back, now inevitably stuck,
She's cut off from her power base of friends.
Attack on nerves.

The conflict tumbled to its destructive end,
the disaster acceptable for one if equally meted to the other.
No way back.
The point of no return.

The dynamics of conflict are not chaotic, haphazard or random. They operate according to certain observable patterns of behaviour, thinking and attitude. Dr Fritz Glasl first recognised this pattern in his formulation of The Conflict Escalator. When observing signs and symptoms of conflict the dynamic forces that operate deep within the conflict and the parties need to be recognised. One incident can give rise to negative feelings, which may foster aggressive behaviour and therefore start a further stage of the conflict. The conflict thus becomes a self-propelling process that generates its own energy. As the conflict escalates, traps multiply which intensify existing tensions. A pathological learning process begins which makes the participants more expert in conflict. Dysfunctional behaviour, which is in fact functional to the conflict, increases. The conflict gathers its own momentum.

One key factor that will influence the dynamics of the conflict is the relative power of the parties to the conflict. If one party has greater power than the other, the conflict is "asymmetrical". The more powerful party can escalate the conflict with less chance of adverse repercussion. On the other hand, the party with less power is taking a greater risk in going up to more intense levels of conflict.

In order to take effective remedial action, an awareness is needed of how the escalation process is working – especially to identify where the points of no return occur. If the conflict is not to escalate or the escalation is to be reversed, the deterioration in behaviour must first be halted. Those involved in the conflict need to be aware of what is really happening so people can see each other again as human beings. They need to accept full responsibility for the consequences of their behaviour on others. This is only possible if those involved experience a "confrontation with reality". This shared insight may be the foundation stone of remedial action.

Someone seeking to help resolve the conflict needs an accurate assessment of the severity of conflict, otherwise serious errors may occur. The real issues may not be addressed appropriately if the severity of the conflict is underestimated, so the conflict will continue to worsen. Even more critically, if the severity of conflict is overestimated, you may overreact. One party may provoke the other into more extreme behaviour.

Figure 1 describes the phases and levels of conflict on the Escalator. There are three main phases, each of which has three levels. The first phase is nervousness and its three levels are discussion, debate and deeds not words. The second phase is neurosis and levels four to six which relate to this phase are fixations, loss of face and strategies of threat. The third and most serious phase is pathological. Levels seven to nine – at the highest level of intensity – are inhumanity, attack on nerves, and no way back.

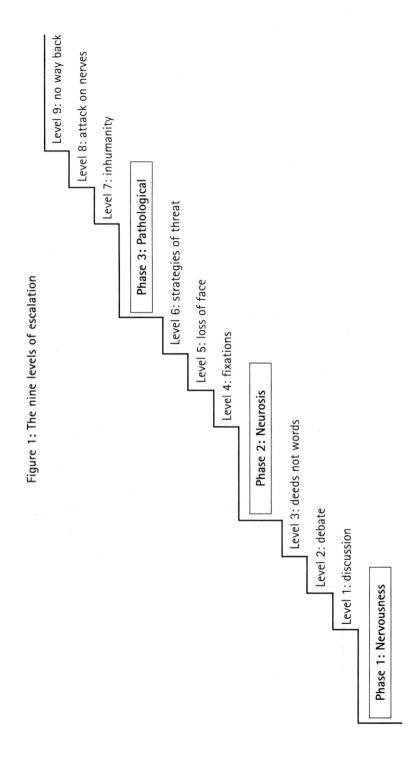

Figure 1: The nine levels of escalation

Level 9: no way back

Level 8: attack on nerves

Level 7: inhumanity

Phase 3: Pathological

Level 6: strategies of threat

Level 5: loss of face

Level 4: fixations

Phase 2: Neurosis

Level 3: deeds not words

Level 2: debate

Level 1: discussion

Phase 1: Nervousness

THE CONFLICT ESCALATOR PHASES

Each level in each phase is characterised by observable patterns of behaviour, thinking and attitude. These are detailed below.

Phase 1: nervousness

This phase relates to occasional, low-level tensions, situations in which co-operation and competition are mixed. There are different interpretations of the problem and how best to deal with it. The parties both focus on the problem and believe a solution will be found. However, the route to each party's preferred solution is being blocked by the other – probably deliberately.

Organizational means can get over these difficulties. Structures or processes can be changed, new methods brought in or more materials or resources used. Careful management may overcome the difficulties by introducing procedures and ways of working which ensure that everyone is clear about norms and standards and that they are adhered to. Even if these changes are made problems and differences continue. Real and latent tensions still get in the way. Antagonisms creep in. People feel touchy and nervous. It becomes increasingly difficult to work together in a rational, controlled way. The other party is believed to be hindering solving the problem. They are becoming more and more obstinate and negative. We now consider each level in the first phase of the escalation process in turn.

Level 1: discussion

The conflict is at a very low level – almost not worth describing as a conflict. Such meetings and conversations take place every day in most organizations. But occasionally things go wrong: in hot conflicts heated discussions may take place. In cold conflicts there may be periods of awkward silence.

"Unfortunate" but uncalculated incidents may lead to overreaction and a build up of tension, at which point the dispute is discussed again. Why worry about this kind of interaction? Because although every one may appear to be suffering no lasting adverse effects they will nonetheless remember hurtful accusations. They may not like it, but they say nothing, biding their time until they can get their own back. They also look out for another possible attack – but this time they will be more careful. The parties become cautious, not taking risks. Any confrontation is normally verbal. Serious clashes are avoided if at all possible. The job to be done, or the shared problem to be solved, is a moderating influence.

Attempts to co-operate and move forward are not made any easier as a result of the residue of caution, friction and tension. Incidental slips may occur and perhaps increase. The arguments go round in circles. People begin to take stances. Proposals are hurried. The crystals of rigid positions start to form. These positions have to be defended, even when they are not specifically being attacked. Others are drawn into the "discussion" which may have started as a dialogue. Each conflicting party tries to persuade others to share their view and take sides.

People feel stuck and occasionally deadlocked. Hard as some try to remove obstacles and hindrances, blockages remain. In fact a party may go so far as to occasionally block the other side. Each side closes ranks and defends its position; subsequently the parties become separated – often physically.

Non-verbal behaviour becomes important, particularly gestures and movements which concentrate attention on a party's arguments but draw attention away from the other's. Views held of each other become distorted. People take on specific and rigid roles in relation to the discussion or spokesperson. A protective barrier is erected that separates the parties psychologically as well as physically: "they are different from us (and as we are right they must be wrong)".

Level 2: debate

Debate is a long and distinguished tradition in many cultures. Debating styles are admired and debating skills are practised and honed to perfection. So-called adversarial systems exist in many areas of public life including the courts and parliament. Debate is a formal contest where the protagonists (for or against a particular point of view) are separated and each argument is presented in turn. There is no spontaneous exchange except to ask questions which are usually designed to undermine the other side. The presentation of the arguments for one case is permeated with attempts to undermine the other, even to the point of ruining the case of an opponent.

The style of a debate is quite formal: rigid, strict rules are observed and procedures are followed. Psychological pressure is exerted through the formal structure of the debate. Unfair tactics become accepted practice. Contradictions and weak points in the other side's arguments are identified and pounced upon with glee. Points are scored and noted at every possible opportunity.

The confrontation is mainly verbal, considered and rational – but with some stronger emotions creeping in. The undercurrent is different from the spoken word. Playing the spoken, civilised behaviour debating game becomes an end in itself rather than a means to an end. The objective of reaching agreement and solving problems recedes. Motives become mixed and uncertainty creeps in about what has been done or said.

One party may still want to co-operate and find a way through, but the other side forces it to become increasingly combative and competitive. It is forced to defend its own convictions, social position and status in the face of attacks from others. As the first party thinks its positions (and the people within it) are the best, they feel the need to defend them. This causes further irritation as each party demonstrates by its own behaviour that it feels itself superior to the other – or at least is committed to equality.

Parties confront each other with dilemmas and false choices "either for or against", "either this or that", "us or them". Common ground, compromise or a middle way, is not believed to be possible. Views appear to be polarised and positions become irreconcilable. Verbal tricks and tactics become more frequent. Everyone seems concerned with impressing the other side or a wider audience rather than listening to alternative arguments. So the debate becomes a competition of logical reasoning; but irrational methods are also used to mislead and confuse others. Personal attacks weaken intellectual positions, exerting emotional pressure on the other side. "Irritators" are used to "wind up" the other side by emphasising the weaknesses in their argument.

Level 3: deeds not words

So far we have been dealing with a "battle of words". At this third level the parties to the conflict become more concerned with actions, or more specifically gaps between what people say and what they do. In a hot conflict this results in more chaotic, furious activity. One party accuses the other. The other defends itself and then makes counter-accusations. In a cold conflict, action is more coolly calculating. Either way each party looks for the worst in the other party – and often gets it!

The parties begin to show their resistance non-verbally, "we are not going to be pushed around". Each side thrusts forward and promotes its own plans, backed up by demonstrations of the strength of will behind its ideas. In effect each is saying "we mean business". The mismatch between words and deeds is a breeding ground for mistrust. Each is quick to point out when the other party is saying one thing and doing another; if there are no obvious signs, some are inferred.

The exchanges become increasingly competitive. Just a hint of co-operation remains. Both sides perhaps realise they still need each other's goodwill to reach an agreement. However, the "agreement" desired must suit only the (winning) party's requirements and must ensure that the other side does not "get away with anything".

The parties become increasingly more reluctant to discuss things with each other and merely present the other side with a *fait accompli*. The attitude is "take it or leave it". Parties to the conflict do not feel obliged to put into action what they have been arguing about, since the other side cannot be trusted; so one must "give as good as one gets". As the discrepancy between verbal and non-verbal messages increases the parties rely more on the perceived significance of non-verbal signals and expressions. Verbal and vocal expression may hide negative intentions and thinking, but non-verbal expressions (such as facial expression, body posture and gestures) may give away exactly what the words are trying to hide. Therefore the parties guess and interpret, usually negatively, the other's non-verbal expressions. In doing so they extrapolate and predict the other's long-term tactics and behaviour. As a result misperceptions, misunderstanding and misinterpretation build up. The parties operate out of a negative "mindset" and see each other in almost entirely negative terms.

Phase 2: neurosis

This phase of the conflict develops into increased persistent friction: where there is the possibility of winning, but the danger of losing. Each party actively looks for opportunities to bend the rules to its own advantage and looks for weaknesses in the rules, using these against the other party. Interaction becomes increasingly competitive; collaboration disappears.

The conflict itself – its outcome and conduct – becomes a major issue. Feelings of resentment or "revenge" increase dramatically. People develop strong, fixed, negative images of each other. They make exaggerated assumptions about each other and what will happen. The underlying problem gets lost. The parties are only concerned about fighting each other. Each party appears to be terrified of the prospect of being seen to lose out or give in. No one concedes anything any more. Threats are made and traded. No one acts with integrity. The conflict has a life of its own and becomes the central feature in the lives of all concerned. We now look at each of the levels in the second phase of escalation.

Level 4: fixations

At this fourth level, the lowest level of the second phase of neurosis, attitudes change from seeing the possibility of a "win/win" to a "win (us)/lose (them)" position. Images become rigid and fixed and the parties imitate and caricature each other, often mimicking voices, walks and attitudes. They make negative stereotypes of others and fix them by frequent repetition. They also build up a distorted but largely positive image of themselves. Everyone becomes obsessive about these images. They try at all costs to protect their reputation and to destroy the reputation of others. As each side vies, they each confirm the expectations of others by acting first.

In a hot conflict this results in extreme statements and behaviour. In cold conflicts behaviour is coldly and calculatingly cynical. Each side sees itself as the personification of all that is good. The other side is described as weak and unworthy. The focus tends to be on intellectual, professional and occupational attitudes and skills; not on negative or positive moral qualities.

The parties are not aware of the distortions taking place. They all believe their images are realistic and fully justified by the "facts". They see what they want to see and create a field of prejudice and fantasy. They know that the other side has an incorrect view of its own human qualities, but it feels like nothing can be done once the conflict has reached this level.

At this level of conflict support is enlisted for each "cause". Each party looks for supporters and tries to build up alliances and coalitions amongst people "like us". They make promises in order to gain support and conduct campaigns to gain sympathy. Doubters are purged from the group. Anyone offering a positive view of the others, or trying to be fair, is seen as weak and is undermined and possibly excluded from future plans. They try to gather supporters who are willing and able to plead their case in finding others who share their values and opinions, but may need some persuasion.

Coalitions come together to show affinity of image and reputation, but they also share the negative and distorted image of the "enemy". Each party attributes qualities to others, whether or not this is justified. All sides point out dangers that don't exist and see non-existent threats. Once a negative image has been built up it must be actively reinforced. Only information that fits into the picture painted filters through, or the information is distorted to reinforce the picture each party has formed. Such coalitions can be formed for protection or as an expression of the need to attack others and thereby to confirm their own image. Under the pressure of negativity and distortion the people involved are inevitably damaged.

Level 5: loss of face

As the attacks mount up and the pressure builds people begin to crack at this second level of the neurosis phase – but they cannot afford to show signs of weakness or be seen to be losing. Pressure is increased on all members of a group to act together. Doubt or uncertainty is expunged, to ritualise and standardise behaviour and to throw out any dissenters. At last the other party is exposed and is seen for what it is and always has been, and always will be. Each ignores the fact that it is being described by others in exactly the same terms.

In a hot conflict this can lead to open, vicious, personal attacks. In a cold conflict the attacks are more subtle and "behind the scenes", but no less damaging. The "face" (i.e. the image, reputation and credibility) has been damaged and exposed. It is like having a disease and being publicly exposed for all to see the condition. At the same time each group's own face has to be maintained or, even better still, enhanced. Enormous energy is required to boost self-image at the same time as countering the threat to "loss of face". Even issues of minor importance affect image. At this level the parties protect and attack pride and false pride.

Each party attacks the other's "face" to prove that they are lying or misleading. The impact on the people involved can be damaging and sometimes devastating. A person's social and human integrity is fundamentally and deeply shocked. In some cultures "losing face" is very potent indeed. Someone's image is a social gift (or loan); a social credit they have gained by their actions. If face is lost social rights may be denied in that group or environment. The individual becomes a social outcast. They feel "de-masked". This disillusionment is particularly difficult to deal with if brought about by the deliberate actions of other people they know. They become isolated. They have been morally disqualified – an intensely damaging experience. Little wonder some people become ill at this stage in a conflict.

After losing face a person will struggle to rehabilitate their dignity. All this takes effort and energy. They may have little energy left for anything else. From this point the parties in a conflict have little choice but to act predictably and rigidly. The conflict and its consequences have become of prime importance. Personal values and self-esteem have to be defended. The best form of defence is probably attack by now.

Level 6: strategies of threat

At this sixth level, the highest level in the neurosis phase, each party threatens the other. The disadvantages of the current and future circumstances for the other party are clearly emphasised. Commitment and certainty are needed if threats are to be made and carried out. Each group has to be seen to be deadly serious because bridges have been burned. Threats are designed to force changes by exerting pressure. In turn each party reacts to whatever the other does – only more strongly. In a hot conflict threats are made forcefully and explicitly. In a cold conflict threats may be veiled, implicit or hidden. In both cases the use of threats becomes predominant. It is argued that no compromise is possible over right and wrong, good or bad. The capacity for violence must be at least mentioned to emphasise commitment to the cause.

When threats are in the air people overreact and plans are made to meet the worst of all possibilities. Crisis meetings and decision-making become the norm. When plans and strategies are being worked out in this crisis atmosphere, space and time contracts. Parties delude themselves that everything can be organised, planned and managed. When their plans are thwarted, or take longer than anticipated, frustration and disappointment increases. Concentrated effort, focused on a world consisting only of the parties directly concerned with the conflict itself, often has the opposite effect to the one sought. When this fails something else must be tried immediately. The pressure and stress of the conflict is added to.

The dynamics of threat are compelling. If the threat is too strong, it loses its effect by appearing ridiculous. If the threat is too weak, it seems inconsequential and even laughable. A threat once carried out is no longer of any use, yet in order to increase its credibility it may be necessary to begin to carry it out – a minor threat carried out to show credibility before a major sanction is imposed. The credibility of a threat requires balancing the demand being made, the threatened punishments or sanctions, the displayed potential to carry out the sanctions, and the expected damage the sanctions may cause to the other side.

If the threatening party becomes too demanding or punishing, more pressure is put on the other side to retaliate in kind. This causes a further escalation. In card games this is called "upping the ante". Threats and counter-threats are traded.

Even if threats are not carried out, people become more defensive. This then becomes aggressive preventative action, so initiating a defend/attack spiral of increasing intensity. Threats that are meant to discourage the other side from further violence have the effect of provoking more violence. People talk of punishment, sanctions and real damage if threats are carried out. If this happens they change the way they view the other side. Permission is given for a new set of conflict targets to be established.

Phase 3: pathological

At this more serious level both parties are concerned with serious, deteriorating, permanent disputes in which the objective is to maximise the other's losses. The parties have become extreme in their language and behaviour. It seems there is nothing they would not do to destroy each other. The people involved lose sight of the reasons for the initial dispute. Others are intent on joining in and making matters worse. The parties are locked in permanent attack from their entrenched positions. Mutual destruction seems to be everyone's aim. Any actions taken only worsen the situation; nothing can be done without the parties feeling it is a threat to their survival. Any norms and standards that have been set to moderate excesses are violated with indifference. The conflict is continued compulsively. People behave in self-destructive ways if it means they can take others down with them. Here are the final levels of the Conflict Escalator.

Level 7: inhumanity

At the lowest level of the pathological phase, preventative, protective actions are paramount. Each party must prepare to defend itself. They must try to disarm the other side while building up their own defences. Thus deciding how best to destroy the other side becomes paramount. Each must convince itself that more radical measures are justified in order to get rid of the other party. To do this, systematic destructive campaigns against the destructive potential of the other party are needed. Achieving any positive outcome from the conflict is abandoned.

Each party's wish to damage the other party is greater than its concern about damaging itself. The emotional destruction of the other party compensates for loss of power and influence: each is now going for the jugular. The parties are helped in this destruction if they can position the other side in their own minds and especially in the minds of others. If each can persuade itself and others that because of the other party's actions, what it represents, its qualities and in its very nature it is somehow a lesser form of humanity, then each feels entirely justified in its subsequent actions. Turning people into monsters legitimises monstrous means being used against them.

Level 8: attack on the nervous system

At this level, the second level of the most intense phase, the only aim is to disable the other side completely. Its power supply must be cut off. A planned attack on the other party's nervous system takes place to cut it off from all sources of support, information and sustenance. Retreat is also blocked. So the other group's supporters cannot cause any damage. They are exposed and isolated and find it impossible to withdraw. They are at the mercy of their attackers.

To carry out an "attack on nerves" campaign a change of emphasis is needed. Preventing the other party from doing damage is no longer enough; it must be damaged. Each group concentrates on the destructive potential and effects of its attacks. The attacks must be specifically targeted at the other party's power base – making sure certain people are not elected to the Board, or spreading rumours and scandals about a colleague to influence management or to get them sacked. The parties would rather risk more damage to themselves than withdraw or capitulate. Behaviour may now be completely irrational, but it makes sense at the intense level to which the conflict has escalated.

Level 9: no way back

The point of no return has been reached at this stage. There is no logic or rationale to what happens. Destructive goals completely dominate. Calculations can be bizarre and irrational. Withdrawal is now a fate worse than self-destruction, if self-destruction will lead to the other side also being destroyed. The conflict has reached a lose/lose situation. Disaster is inevitable, but as long as the destruction is mutual some satisfaction can be derived.

The levels of violence know no limits. Both sides are so morally weakened that their actions are limited. This does not stop them escalating the threats and increasing the intensity of action. The conflict can only end with the collapse of the other side. All buttons of destruction are pressed at once.

USING THE ESCALATOR IN YOUR LIVING CASE STUDY

The Escalator is an important tool in helping you understand how serious your living case study conflict has become. As seen above, this is vital in deciding which conflict resolution strategy you subsequently choose. There are two Activities that will help you to assess the seriousness of the conflict by using the Escalator model in your living case study conflict.

The first of these Activities provides a summary of the main features of the Conflict Escalator to assist in assessing what stage the conflict is at. Turn now to:

ACTIVITY 5 Page 156

After you have completed this Activity, move on to the "moments of truth" exercise, which provides a different approach to establishing the level of conflict in your case study and should confirm your findings in Activity 5. Turn now to:

ACTIVITY 6 Page 159

6. First Steps Towards Resolution

IN THIS CHAPTER: Establishing a framework for approaching the conflict. First principles and the beginnings of action.

Contents

6 First Steps Towards Resolution

So far we have analysed the nature of conflict (hot or cold), the temperaments of individuals and groups involved, the process and levels of conflict escalation. Before moving on to the particular approaches, skills and techniques needed to resolve conflict (Chapters 7, 8 and 9), we will first re-cap on our analytical framework. In particular, how this framework suggests first steps towards formulating a plan for resolution.

WHAT KIND OF CONFLICT IS IT?

Hot conflict

When aiming to resolve a hot conflict, sharing information to analyse accurately what is going on is important preparation. The parties to a conflict are likely to appreciate the exchange of data and information. They like matters to be open, and enjoy arguments and debate. But the information might be sensationalised and used to escalate the conflict.

Each party will be keen to meet the other to "have things out". Therefore a strategy that involves thrashing things out in meetings could prove successful, so long as the strategic aims of resolving the conflict are kept firmly in mind. The best way to resolve a hot conflict is to cool it down. The conflict needs to be made less hectic and more measured. That is what the plan for resolution needs to focus on.

Cold conflict

In cold conflicts parties will strongly resist sharing information. They would prefer to keep things quiet and under the surface. The pretence that nothing is wrong is maintained. If the problem is admitted, they feel that looking at it more closely serves no purpose. Nothing can be done to resolve it anyway.

There is little point organizing a meeting if the parties sit in sullen silence and remain as defensive, protective and uncommunicative as before. It may be more effective to approach matters differently. For example, quietly and gently working with individuals to give them encouragement and support may be a more effective strategy. So the first steps in resolving a cold conflict are to start to convince people that something *can* be done to resolve the conflict. They need to question their feelings of being trapped. This may improve their self-esteem so that they can resolve the conflict.

WHAT IS THE LEVEL OF ESCALATION?

Depending on the level of escalation you are dealing with, conflict resolution can take a number of forms, moving from prevention at lower levels to integrated resolution at more serious levels. These different forms are outlined in Figure 2, giving indications of what is required at each stage.

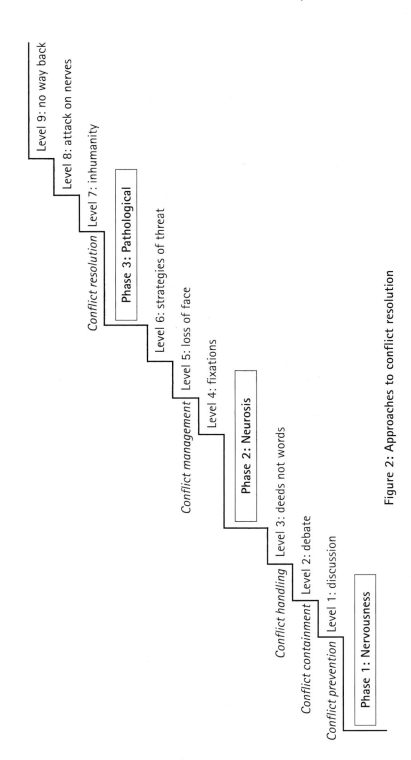

Figure 2: Approaches to conflict resolution

Approaches to phase 1 conflicts

Conflict prevention: objectives include preventing the conflict escalating in the first place; identifying the early signs; and taking appropriate decisive action.

Conflict containment: objectives include keeping the lid on the conflict; stopping it at early stages; creating a pause; moderating behaviour so that things do not get any worse; dealing with difficulties and tensions but also concentrating on the need to re-establish relationships; exploring what is going wrong and why; examining the problems for faults and difficulties.

Conflict handling: objectives include taking more direct action to bring the parties back to a position where more or less normal relationships can be re-established; limiting the worst excesses of the conflict whilst at the same time taking clear, positive steps to deal with the conflict issues; closely monitoring the circumstances, bringing in an element of peace-keeping.

Approaches to phase 2 conflicts

Conflict management: objectives include carefully planned and controlled conflict management - processes established that involve a number of related and integrated activities; setting rules and establishing boundaries; bringing in extra resources when required; clarifying roles and getting agreement for a more disciplined, managed approach; some elements of peace-making.

Approaches to phase 3 conflicts

Conflict resolution: objectives include applying more inclusive and longer-term strategies; drawing up pre-determined plans for conflict resolution in all its aspects; peace-making as well as peace-keeping; total management of the situation; allocating time and resources to conflict resolution; time tabling and programming conflict resolution; sequencing and structuring all elements, including legal considerations.

To calculate the level of escalation in your living case study conflict turn to:

Now find the level on Figure 2. You will see the type of conflict resolution appropriate to the level of the conflict you intend to resolve. So, if your living case study conflict is presently at Phase 2 Level 6 of the Escalator Model, your best approach to resolution is conflict management. What follows are checklists of the aims of each conflict resolution approach

CORE PRINCIPLES IN APPROACHING CONFLICT RESOLUTION

- Conflicts are more about people than problems.

- Conflicts create their own field of energy. They take on a life of their own, outside the control and beyond the normal consciousness of the parties themselves.

- Conflicts tend to get worse if left alone; therefore positive and determined action is needed to resolve them. There is a reducing chance of improving relationships and de-escalating the conflict as people take more serious action; acting early is best.

- The ultimate aim of conflict resolution is to enable the parties themselves to build up the capacity to help themselves.

- Involve the parties themselves in as many of the conflict resolution activities as possible – begin by passing on a more complete understanding of what the conflict is about.

- Once a strategy and process of conflict resolution has been determined (in outline at least), trust the process!

- Ensure that any analysis of the phase and level of escalation of the conflict is as accurate as possible. If the seriousness of the conflict is over-estimated the effects of any interventions could make the conflict worse. The parties could decide that the conflict is more serious than they realised, and then take more severe and damaging action. If the seriousness of the conflict is under-estimated any interventions are likely to be perceived as too weak or inconsequential. The credibility of the person who is attempting the conflict resolution is damaged and there may be an over-reaction to events, which will confirm that the conflict is more serious than appears. This can happen in cold conflicts where a great deal is happening under the surface.

★

In preparing to try to resolve a conflict, consideration needs to be given to changing behaviour, attitudes and perceptions. All three must change over a period of time. This is what characterises a developmental approach to resolving conflict. Changes in only one area may not last and will not offer the maximum opportunities for learning for all participants.

Changing behaviour

It is assumed – often quite rightly if the conflict has reached serious levels of escalation – that some outside force is needed to stop the parties inflicting damage on each other. So law and order approaches are used in conflict resolution, instituting "cease-fires", stopping the parties acting in certain ways and controlling and disciplining (sometimes by punishing). This may be necessary as an interim measure and work for a while, but damaging behaviour will be resumed as soon as the controlling influence is reduced.

In preparing the aims of your conflict resolution strategy you should first consider which behaviours you want to change and how you think they might be influenced. The psychologist Skinner (1904-1990) said, "Behaviour is shaped and maintained by its consequences". His theory is that behaviour is conditioned and influenced by rewards, reprimands or punishment. These "shape and maintain" your behaviour patterns.

The same could be said of people's behaviour in conflicts. As we have described, the positive and negative interactions with others "decide" how someone will react with and to other people. Positive (or "rewarded") behaviour from others may mean that a person feels associated with a group; negative (or "reprimanded") behaviour from others may mean that they feel rejected by a group. Therefore, the person takes the side of those whose behaviour towards them is positive. But the people in *both* groups believe they behave positively, while in fact treat each other negatively.

Each group has "key players" – ringleaders who set the mood through their dominant behaviour. As an essential first step, the key players' behaviour must be regulated or altered to change the circumstances as a whole. The following is a list of some behaviour you may be experiencing in your living case study:

- Dismissive comments
- Lack of listening
- Flare-ups
- Frozen sulks and silences
- Excluding people from meetings
- Challenging comments
- Sarcastic or insulting comments
- Physical positioning at meetings
- Ignoring others.

A *marked* change does not, however, always necessarily mean a *large* change. Sometimes a small change can alter the whole picture. A direct method would be to address the person face to face and ask them to change their behaviour; indirect methods include rearranging a seating plan at a meeting, or changing the order in which people speak, or changing the venue.

When there is evidence to suggest there has been a marked change in behaviour you can move on to changing attitudes and perceptions. It is as well to prepare your approach to these later stages at the outset or very early on.

Changing attitudes

Attitudes harden because of lack of respect and a breakdown of trust. Each party feels that their attitude towards others (and themselves) is justified. It is little use, therefore, appealing to the parties to "trust" each other and to treat each other better. The parties concerned will undoubtedly see this approach as moralising. Such appeals may work for a while, but rarely have lasting positive effects, particularly whilst behaviour may continue to reinforce hardened attitudes and negative perceptions.

"Attitude" can be defined as a "positive or negative feeling about some person, object or issue" (Petty and Cacioppo, psychologists, 1981). For the purposes of conflict resolution it is the stance a person takes against another. In a conflict this is usually negative (e.g. distrust, lack of respect, dislike, suspicion, superiority and insolence). Attitude has a motivating effect on behaviour: if a person profoundly distrusts another, the other person can do little to win any trust.

Changing perceptions

An early sign of conflict is that people begin to see each other more negatively. On the other hand, they see themselves in an increasingly positive light. As the conflict escalates these views become more distorted. Just getting people to see each other differently will not work if attitudes have hardened and behaviour still reinforces the distorted images, no matter how sophisticated the psychological methods used.

Many perceptions people have of themselves and others are inaccurate or flawed. Partial and imperfect views can result. How perceptions developed needs to be established. Then what needs to be done to inculcate positive perception needs to be identified. Once this change in perception has been achieved, it is possible to move on to the problem itself.

★

To summarise, in planning your approach to resolve a conflict you will need to decide the type and level of conflict. You will also need to decide your objectives and to understand the underlying dynamics of the conflict. Finally you will need to identify a starting point. This is likely to be seeking a marked change in behaviour. This can be followed by seeking changes in attitudes and perceptions. You can then seek to address some key questions about the conflict:

- Do I really know what is going on?
- What are the most important underlying influences at work?
- What is it really all about?
- Where is the conflict going?
- How can we stop it?
- What needs to happen now?

Once you have answered these questions above, formulated objectives for the conflict resolution and made a plan, you will then need to decide on the roles that need to be played for resolution and who should play them. It is to the issues of roles in resolution that we turn in Chapter 7.

Before doing this, consider some of the factors in planning your first steps towards resolution.

ACTIVITY 8 Page 174

7. Roles for Resolution

IN THIS CHAPTER: Planning appropriate modes of intervention for a particular conflict.

Contents

7 Roles for Resolution

By now you have the answers to the questions:

- Is the conflict hot or cold?
- What level of escalation has been reached?
- What are the first steps to conflict resolution?

Answers to these questions will indicate the role(s) that will need to be played in the conflict resolution itself. In some cases the role(s) will be carried out by protagonists to the conflict, but the role(s) may also be carried out by third parties. As a general principle, the protagonists themselves should take on as much resolution as they can. Even if a third party is used initially, their aim should be to enable the parties in the conflict to internalise this activity and carry it out themselves. The aim of this approach – a developmental strategy – is eventually to resolve the underlying problems that have triggered the conflict as well as the conflict itself. In the process the parties can learn to express themselves clearly and perhaps establish better relationships for the long term. All parties are responsible for resolving the conflict and accountable for the results. If the parties must continue to work together a developmental approach is essential. They have a chance to learn from the conflict by addressing the underlying issues, provided the time, commitment and resources are invested into building sustainable long-term relationships.

A developmental strategy to conflict resolution involves an act of determined will directed towards reconciliation, healing and shared responsibility. It involves bringing each party to the stage of being able to sit down together and sort out their difficulties by talking about them.

The nature and dynamics of the conflict will be a guide to deciding roles that need to be played. Different roles, strategies and activities will be needed if the conflict has escalated to a serious level by comparison to those necessary in a low level conflict. If the parties prefer a "hot" approach the conflict resolution will have to mirror this to be effective.

The three Escalator phases also have an influence on the roles played. The roles are "moderator", "facilitator", "therapist" and "mediator/arbitrator". Figure 3 shows the phases of the Escalator to which each role is best suited. In outline, the roles are as follows:

- Phase 1 needs a moderator or a facilitator to help with the conflict resolution process.
- Phase 2 initially needs a therapist, then a moderator/facilitator to de-escalate the conflict.
- Phase 3 needs arbitration or mediation, followed by a therapeutic process, and then the moderator/facilitator.

Most effective managers could play any of these roles – although sometimes experts may be needed. These roles should be carried out in a *downward* direction, thus reversing the escalation of the conflict. Sometimes roles overlap or more than one role is needed at a particular time.

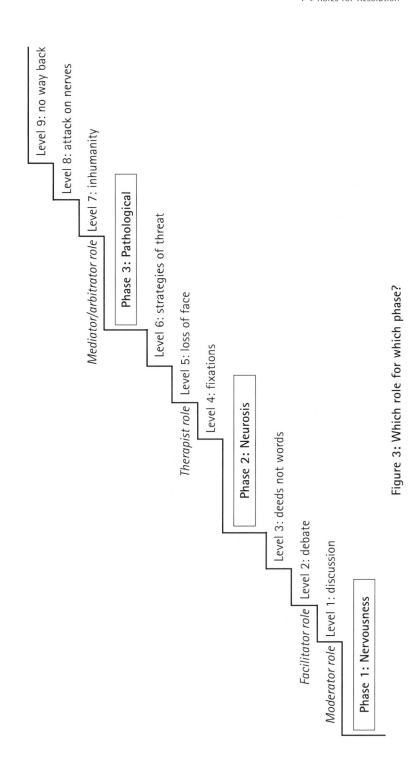

Figure 3: Which role for which phase?

THE "MODERATOR"

In the early stages of a conflict, usually at Levels 1 (discussion) and 2 (debate) of the Conflict Escalator, the moderator role is the most effective. The role will probably be taken on by one of the protagonists to the conflict itself. The moderator clarifies misconceptions and misunderstandings as they arise; introduces ways of moderating language and behaviour; prevents skirmishes from turning into battles; and repairs any damage preventing it being carried over to the next meeting. Moderators can make suggestions. The following statements reflect a moderating role:

> *"I think we're all getting overheated and in danger of forgetting we all work towards the same ends. I suggest we take a break and continue in fifteen minutes"* .

> *"I think we're in danger of becoming too personal, I'd prefer us all to stick to the facts".*

> *"It seems to me that we're going round in circles and not really facing up to the hidden issues. I'd like to suggest that we first of all check our genuine interest in resolving this problem".*

In moderation summarising how far things have (or have not) moved and crediting all parties with their contributions are useful techniques. Moderators can also identify different processes or approaches to resolving the conflict, for example:

- Having some discussion separately before coming together.

- Having a few minutes' general and personal conversation before beginning a meeting to remind people of the "whole" human beings involved rather than the one-sided professional view.
- Showing similes or metaphors rather than only considering wordy reports.

Each party may have its own "natural" moderator. The moderators on each side are the ones that will inspire most trust from their opposing side. They often emerge spontaneously and can be encouraged to take a leading role. Moderators are most effective early on in a conflict. If they only become visible at Levels 4 and 5 they will be branded a weak link and sidelined.

THE "FACILITATOR"

It is difficult but sometimes possible for one of the protagonists to perform this role. A facilitator operating at Level 3 and Level 4 conflicts however will most usually be a third party, perhaps someone from the same department or organization but with sufficient independence from all the protagonists to be seen as objective and impartial (as to Third Party roles, see further below). Even at low levels of conflict the parties find it increasingly difficult to keep the relationship stable and to get things done. A facilitator helps them to do little things, and some of the bigger ones, which the conflict has diverted them from.

Differences at this early stage tend to be about words, ideas and opinions. Thoughts are misinterpreted, information and "facts" are disputed or ignored, ideas are expressed badly. Strong feelings arise about any discrepancy or when views are challenged. The facilitator helps people to get out of their extreme and inflexible positions. Any undercurrents of real disagreement can be brought to the surface. Unexpressed concerns and intentions can be made explicit. The facilitator questions the parties to establish if they really meant what they said (or wrote), to check whether the message has been accurately understood and perhaps to check the underlying intentions and motives.

These methods depend on everyone being rational and willing to pause to look behind current events. This can be difficult during a discussion. It demands self-discipline. The facilitator cannot be forced on the parties; at a minimum they must accept that this is a useful role. Dependence on a facilitator may be reduced over time. The parties may internalise the role and carry it out themselves.

Each incident needs examination in greater depth by both parties together with the facilitator to uncover the underlying issues. The facilitator helps to explore the distortions which have taken hold. They may also give more direct guidance and specific instruction. They stand outside the conflict, at a distance from all parties. The parties to the conflict must hand over some authority and control, and be prepared to work to the facilitator's instructions.

THE "THERAPIST"

As with the role of facilitator, the role of therapist could be undertaken by another manager or specialist within the organization. The term therapist is usually associated with psychotherapy and health. Yet there is no better word to describe this role. At this stage the people involved are too busy with their conflict to carry out their day-to-day tasks. Relationships are degenerating. More importantly people are being damaged. This damage needs to be repaired before progress towards normality can be achieved. Damage limitation is necessary if the conflict is not to degenerate even further.

The activities of the therapist in this context are preventative and curative. Remedial work requires a concentrated effort to identify the nature of the problem and to encourage action to build up confidence, re-establish self-esteem and help people come to terms with deeper feelings of guilt, shame and anger which often underpin the bravado of conflict.

Therapy, coaching and counselling by experts is often carried out separately with individuals and each group. By understanding the conflict the therapist – without becoming personally immersed – can help people to understand their own circumstances at a deeper level. This in itself can be the first step towards remedying the conflict.

THE "ARBITRATOR/MEDIATOR"

If conflicts have escalated to Phase 3 then a different type of conflict resolution and a specialist role are needed. An arbitrator is almost always an outside, third party role, whereas a mediator can be a less remote (independent) figure but one who performs a definite outsider/external function in a more informal go-between role. An arbitrator/mediator must be well known enough, and experienced enough, to have gained respect. Someone in another team or department of the same organization might be appropriate.

In order to transfer a conflict to mediation or arbitration the parties may be required to re-define the conflict in terms of objective disagreements. The subjective element is put to one side, creating a breathing space for parties to argue their objective case. It would be a cease-fire of conflict behaviour and a break point in conflict escalation. Arbitration can then be a platform for further conflict resolution efforts.

Arbitrators and mediators may be appointed as part of an existing formal procedure or may have to participate because of their position in the organization. Often a more senior manager is called upon to make an arbitration decision when there is a conflict between staff. Once the conflict is handed over to an arbitrator, the parties become passive and only react to the moves and direction of the arbitrator.

Arbitration only penetrates superficially into people's internal world. Subjective and group dynamic issues are largely left unaddressed. Arbitration rarely produces preventative or remedial effects but can offer a way out of a complete deadlock at the most serious levels of escalation, especially when threats have destroyed any basis for co-operation.

For arbitration to be effective the arbitrator must have the power to enforce a decision on the parties, and to have agreement that it will be adhered to. In this sense the conflict has not been resolved, merely sidelined. Mediation, then therapy and facilitation should immediately follow arbitration if a lasting effect is to be achieved.

When the parties to a conflict believe that no basis exists for joint resolution, then a mediator can do a useful job. A mediator is essentially a negotiator or a go-between, who tries to negotiate between the parties to help them build up trust. Everyone must trust the third party, accepting his or her neutrality and independence. This trust in the outsider has to compensate for the total lack of trust between the parties at the later stages of conflict. A mediator has to accept that the parties will not initially be completely open. The mediator may be confronted with the same dilemma the parties themselves are struggling with. On the one hand, the mediator selects information, carefully watches the tactical moves of the parties and tries to communicate when the parties can no longer do so in meetings; on the other hand, the mediator must be able to influence and pressurise the parties. Eventually, therefore, the parties may reach a stage when they begin to do their own mediation.

THE THIRD PARTY ROLE

A third party to conflict, whether a facilitator, therapist, arbitrator or mediator, is expected and required to be much more directive and controlling than in other training, development and learning situations, although learning is the ultimate aim of a conflict resolution process. In conflicts they will be working against the grain in many ways, understanding the power of the forces at work within the conflict and counter-acting them; telling the parties what needs to be done and avoided at each stage of the resolution process (which they have determined in consultation with the parties); and monitoring closely whether the conditions to aid resolution are working. They will also monitor whether rules, guidelines and limits laid down and agreed on are being adhered to. If the rules are being broken there should be immediate reference to an open system of review and evaluation, examining the causes of such a breakdown and taking remedial action.

The higher the level of escalation, the more directive the third party has to become. Arbitration, for example, is a formal, strict, quasi-judicial, directed, decision-making process. The success of mediation often depends on whether the parties stick rigidly to a prescribed, stylistic series of steps, demanding patience and stamina. Therapy demands discipline with the third party in charge of the process. Nonetheless, everyone should participate with the objective of shared responsibility for outcomes.

Facilitation is less visibly directive, though the facilitator still requires a clear idea of what they are doing and why. In addition the trust and agreement of the parties to the steps being proposed is necessary: at least that they are well thought out, purposeful and relevant – even if the initial reaction of one of the parties is negative. Skills and techniques appropriate to these roles are discussed in Chapters 8 and 9.

A third party carrying through a longer-term conflict resolution process with the active participation of the parties involved will need to switch focus and change roles a number of times. These changes in emphasis should be carefully programmed, not to suit the third party, but to ensure that the protagonists experience the process of conflict resolution as a natural progression. This is even more difficult to achieve if more than one third party is active in the process, which is often the case (e.g. when an arbitrator hands over to a mediator).

If the conflict parties know what is going on, who is involved and what role they are playing, and what is expected of them they are more likely to support (or at least not sabotage) the conflict resolution. Their active and conscious involvement will also reinforce the handing over of responsibility for resolving the conflict from the third party to the conflict parties themselves. If the parties know more about what is going on they are likely to take on some of these responsibilities themselves, thus turning the process into one of learning and development for themselves.

Going through the process of making this decision is most immediately useful if you intend to play an active role in your living case study – or even if you want to bring in others, either from inside the organization or outsiders. In the longer term you may wish to consider playing a conflict resolution role in areas other than your own, in other sections or departments, or even other organizations in the same sector.

Carrying out the role

Working with the positive elements in the situation

A minimum requirement is recognition by all concerned that conflict resolution is necessary. The initial focus should be on the positive (or at least not entirely negative) people.

Contracting with the parties

A third party needs to make clear to the protagonists what they will be doing, when and how. This may mean describing respective roles in some detail and gaining agreement for what will be done. This may mean imposing a certain degree of discipline and control where these qualities are absent. When this happens protagonists may not like it and may try to stop it. In such circumstances a previously drawn up agreement will be helpful. The principle of making a clear agreement applies whether someone from inside the organization or an outsider undertakes the role.

Integrity

The third party needs to stick to their principles and be honest. This will be difficult, especially if they come under personal attack from the parties.

Persuasiveness

Being right is often not enough. The third party also has to be persuasive and try to influence people to move in directions they are not used to. This is especially true when using insights and information gained during the phase of investigation and data collection. It is one thing to know what is going on, but quite another to persuade, say, protagonists of what is happening and why.

Objectivity

Many attempts will be made to draw a third party into personal squabbles or persuade them that a particular point of view is right. A third party may have personal views on all these issues; if so, they will have to be kept quiet. An open mind is best. The only information that should be used is that which helps others to understand and act.

Confidentiality

It is often valuable to make an agreement (again, perhaps a written one) with all the parties to keep confidentiality. Nothing should be repeated outside without the expressed permission of the parties themselves. If the third party is seen to be sticking to those standards there may be a better chance of the protagonists also relying less on rumour, stories and half-truths.

Know yourself

A third party should be aware of their own personal strengths and weaknesses: where they can operate confidently and where they feel less secure. It is invariably better to work with a colleague in conflict resolution. This helps to construct a balance of skills, give feedback and, most importantly, support when things get difficult. Working with others may not always be possible, in which case the third party will have to act as their own speaking partner through a process of constant questioning, review and evaluation.

Consider the role appropriate to your conflict. Turn now to:

8. Skills

IN THIS CHAPTER: Questions,
approaches and points to consider at
different stages of resolution.

Contents

8 Skills

So by now you have answers to the questions:

- Is the conflict hot or cold?
- What phase of conflict are we in? What level of escalation have we reached?
- What are the first steps to be taken?
- What roles need to be played in the conflict resolution?
- Are the roles to be played by a party to the conflict or by a third party?

This chapter sets out the skills required for the roles discussed in Chapter 7. A third party will often have gained the skills and experience needed during their career or personal life, and this is needed if they are to gain the respect of the parties, particularly where arbitration is involved. Along with experience and practised skill it may be a question of "track record" in a particular sector, qualifications, status and position which helps build up the necessary credibility.

Different third party roles will call for different skills. In carrying out a therapeutic role the skill profile required may overlap with, for example, counselling, welfare, psychology and social work. Being a facilitator may require using common sense, sensitivity to events and empathy. Skills overlap strongly with personal qualities and interests. Acceptability to the conflicting parties is a minimum requirement for a third party, although this acceptance may be grudging and reluctant. Conflict parties will also look for a commitment to conflict resolution in the third party, as well as impartiality, sensitivity and insight.

The moderator and facilitator need the skill of reflecting as well as the ability to see the overview. The therapist needs the skill to support but also to confront and challenge. The arbitrator/mediator need the skills associated with inspiring others and getting things moving. Central to each pair of skills and qualities, which are the opposite of each other, is the need to bring things into balance as illustrated in Figure 4 below. Balancing these skills and qualities is the ultimate skill in effective conflict resolution.

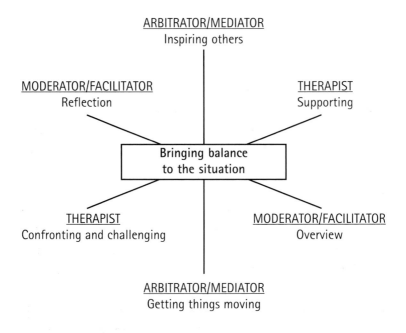

Figure 4: Skills required for each role

All the skills and qualities listed above can be divided between "hard" skills and "soft" skills. Hard skills are confrontation and challenge, inspiring others and getting things moving. Soft skills are supporting, reflecting and overview. Thus, the arbitrator/mediator roles of inspiring others and getting things moving can be balanced by the moderator/facilitator roles of reflection and overview respectively. The therapist can balance supporting and confronting/challenging roles. The softer roles may come in useful as the conflict resolution reaches each new critical stage. These roles are also effective at the beginning of the conflict resolution; a harder approach can be brought in later once the parties have been appeased. Beginning with a hard approach may make it much more difficult to bring in a softer element later.

REFLECTING

Reflecting means searching for the inner essentials of the conflict: what are the core mechanisms that are driving it and what are the dynamics of escalation? Reflecting helps in understanding and learning from events. Past circumstances are recalled and examined for their significance. Particular incidents should be selected and considered in detail. Alternatively, a series of events over a longer period can be mapped out in order to see the bigger picture. Reflecting is non-judgmental: events can speak for themselves before jumping to conclusions.

Observed behaviour, actual events and real feelings expressed by those who have or have had these feelings should always be the basis for reflection. Above all continuous reflection and evaluation is an integral part of working towards a resolution. Appropriate questions would include:

- Has this happened before?
- Have you thought or felt like this before?
- Could what we have learned from the past help us now?

OVERVIEWING

An essential skill in conflict resolution is the ability to see the connection between events, how one thing leads to another (over time) and, particularly in the case of the escalation process how past, present and future are interlinked. Those who are directly involved need to make their own connections and see their own patterns. The process can be assisted by such questions as:

- Does this happen often?
- What pattern is repeated?
- What does it all add up to?
- How would I sum it all up?
- What does this mean to me?

SUPPORTING THOSE INVOLVED

Support requires *displayed* care and support. It begins with paying attention to others and giving them time, listening (with openness and interest), observing and monitoring. Being over-protecting or smothering is not supporting.

There is an important difference between "sympathy" and "empathy". "Sympathy" is showing pity to someone: "isn't it awful" and "how do you put up with that?" "Empathy" is putting yourself in the other person's shoes so that you can understand what it is they are feeling under the circumstances. "I can understand why you feel that way" and "I can see how that might make you feel angry". By showing empathy you are *relating* to the other person and their situation, rather than simply *agreeing* with them and reinforcing their negative outlook.

Feedback – positive and negative – is also an important way of giving support. Positive feedback indicates respect for the other person, genuinely valuing their contribution. Negative feedback must be handled sensitively so that it is supportive and not soul-destroying. One way of balancing between positive and negative feedback is to give more than one item of positive feedback items for every negative one, and always to give the positive ones first.

CHALLENGING AND CONFRONTING

Sometimes people needed to be faced with issues they have been avoiding; such avoidance is helping the conflict to take hold. Conflicts thrive on distortions, illusions, and fantasies.

Confronting and challenging someone or a whole group requires a recognition of the need for such action and taking the opportunity when it arises. A higher level of risk and initiative is needed. The timing, style and methodology of confronting and challenging are of the essence. The outcome may be uncertain, the reaction questionable. The person challenging needs to be courageous but not reckless, challenging but not attacking. Questions you might ask are:

- How can you be saying (b) when you also agree with (a)?
- How compatible are (a) and (b)?
- What do you really want to get out of the conflict?
- What is in this for you?

INSPIRING

The skill of inspiring and energising others is essential when people are unable to find a positive way forward. Some of the ways of doing it include the following:

- Probe the future, envision what might be, choose a direction to go in, set goals and make plans.
- Examine people's internal state as well as external events, illustrate how people have become victims of the conflict, refuse to allocate individual blame but admit collective responsibility.
- Bring in new elements, find alternative courses of action, show new options and possibilities.
- Describe circumstances including the conflict in new and objective ways.
- Show examples from elsewhere of what has been done and what can be done.
- Build up the will to try again if previous attempts have failed.

Above all concentrate on what can be *done now* to help matters in the future. Set objectives, allocate responsibilities and timescales, and pose questions such as:

- What do you want to do about the situation?

- What will be the consequences and implications of doing this, especially for others?
- What obstacles and barriers can you see?
- How can we overcome them?

GETTING THINGS MOVING

In many conflicts the underlying essentials have become stuck despite an apparent flurry of superficial activity. Getting people moving in resolving the conflict includes working with their inner motivation, commitment and energy.

The pace should not be dictated by others. People can feel stressed because they are being forced to operate out of tune with their natural rhythm. People need to be brought together, by arranging meetings or contact points, creating "meeting" possibilities and re-establishing personal contact and connections (especially in cold conflicts). The sort of questions that need to be posed include:

- Can you give examples of what has been happening?
- What sort of things are you afraid might happen?
- What are all the possible things we could do?
- What is stopping us?

Look for practical implications and bring in examples. Move the discussion on if it becomes stuck. Change the mood and the atmosphere. Sometimes well chosen humour, lightness and levity - especially with empathy, bathos or irony - is one way of bringing appropriate movement.

KEEPING A BALANCE

The skills and qualities outlined above need to be balanced. In keeping a balance between all the other qualities, the process of conflict resolution must be monitored carefully. At any one time different qualities are needed. Sometimes more challenging is needed, sometimes less support. Sometimes taking an overview is required, at others getting things moving is needed. Reflecting on what has happened may be necessary on some occasions, whilst inspiring others may be more appropriate. Being in close touch with what is happening, how people are feeling, what should come next and having a sense of how things are going overall will help to keep a balance. The person helping to resolve the conflict must have an awareness of their own role and the contribution they are making. Decisions about what is needed do not have to be made by the person seeking resolution alone. Some of the protagonists to the conflict can be involved by questions such as:

- Have we had enough of this?
- Where are we now?
- Are you happy with what is going on?
- What should we do now?
- Is there anything missing?
- What should or next step be?

9. Techniques

IN THIS CHAPTER: Practical methods of changing behaviour, attitude and perception.

Contents

9 Techniques

So now you have the answers to the questions:
- Is the conflict hot or cold?
- What phase of conflict are we in? What level of escalation have we reached?
- What are the first steps to be taken?
- What roles need to be played in the conflict resolution?
- Are the roles to be played by a party to the conflict or by a third party?
- What skills will be needed in the conflict resolution?

But skills are no use unless they are applied. Skills need to be shown in behaviours. As we have said, if conflict resolution is to be effective and to be a learning experience, all parties need to change, acquiring new skills and behaving in new and different ways.

ASSERTIVENESS

Conflict resolution needs decisiveness and assertiveness. The parties to the conflict need to be encouraged to be more assertive (and therefore less passive or aggressive). Assertiveness as a group of skills and approaches was first developed in the United States to help patients regain their confidence. (In the context of work, see also Fritchie and Melling's *Business of Assertiveness*.)

Basic assertion

Basic assertion is saying what you think, feel or want in a straightforward and direct way. Examples of statements of basic assertion are:

> *"I think we should increase our staff."*
>
> *"Yesterday's meeting was not well received, I'd like to discuss it."*
>
> *"I feel that three days is reasonable."*
>
> *"The figures are not good, I believe we need to talk."*
>
> *"I need to set up a meeting this week."*
>
> *"This product looks good, I think it will be successful."*

When the other party is also able to state their feelings, thoughts or needs in a reasonable way, you can be fairly certain of a balanced, fair and equal relationship. In a hot conflict, basic assertion can reduce emotional escalation at an early stage.

Responsive assertion

Responsive assertion encourages others to speak about their views, feelings or thoughts, not to catch them unawares. Examples of statements of responsive assertion are:

> *"So far we have heard from both planning and administration about how the new guidelines are affecting them. Bill, I'd like to ask you to give us your*

views about how they are affecting delivery."

*"We've discussed the restructuring at some length now
and there seems to be broad agreement that the second
plan is the most appropriate one. Before we make a
final decision, it is important to be clear about the
support this decision can expect. I'd like to start with
you, Bill: what do you think?'*

Sometimes quiet or passive people appear to be silent
observers with little or no involvement in events around
them. Their understanding cannot be checked or their
views sought without putting them on the spot.
Sometimes this silence stems from a lack of confidence or
a difficulty in finding the "right" words or the "right"
time to say them. However, some silent people are more
damaging and these "silent saboteurs" stay quiet whilst a
decision is being taken or a difficult issue is being
discussed, and then speak negatively about it in private or
dissociate themselves from subsequent events.

Empathetic assertion

Empathy means having an understanding of (not pity for)
others, so empathetic assertion begins with the view,
position, thoughts or feelings of the other person,
followed by your own thoughts, position or feelings,
linked by non-emotive word(s) like "however" or
"nevertheless" or "on the other hand". Examples of
empathetic assertion are:

*"From what you've said it's clear that you feel very
strongly about bringing forward the delivery date.
However, I think that it is worth considering. I*

suggest we make a final decision next week when we'll have more opportunity to assess the full impact."

"I can see that you are angry about the way the meeting went and you think that it's all down to me. I agree it wasn't a good meeting and I could have handled it better: however, I think there were a number of hidden agendas at play. I'd like to find out a little more about them and meet again tomorrow morning."

This is particularly appropriate in organizations that place a high priority on valuing people. A short direct statement is made about what the person speaking would like to happen next. The statement needs to begin with a demonstration that you have listened, heard and understood others' views.

Discrepancy assertion

Discrepancy assertion is used in situations where contradictory messages are received. Examples of discrepancy assertion are:

"Earlier this month we agreed that I would be given additional resources to manage the end-of-the-month figures. Today I got a memo from you saying we had to cut back on staff numbers. I'd like to be clear about how this affects our first agreement."

"At my staff appraisal we both agreed I was taking on too much work and it was causing me a lot of stress. In the last few weeks my department has been given several additional new projects. I'd like to discuss the implications of this extra work."

"During the meeting you made a number of negative comments about the performance of my department. This afternoon, privately you said it wasn't really so bad. I'm confused about your real position, so I'd like to meet and clarify it."

In a fast paced, fast changing work scenario, mixed messages are a frequent by-product. Guesswork or assumptions can lead to misunderstanding. Discrepancy assertion helps to clear up misunderstandings before they become serious difficulties. It is also a useful way to point out inconsistencies in behaviour without blaming or being accusatory. People can then move nearer to a workable compromise. With discrepancy assertion it is important to be objective, pointing out known facts and avoiding emotional language.

Negative feelings assertion

Negative feelings assertion is saying what is happening and how you feel about it in a constructive way. Examples of negative feelings assertions are:

"When you shout and lose your temper with me it becomes hard to listen to what you have to say. I feel upset when you do it so I'd like to take it more quietly."

"Each time you arrive at the meeting unprepared it means we have to recap for your benefit only. I feel irritated about this. In future I would ask you to prepare in advance."

"When you go silent and turn away it is difficult for me to understand the cause. I feel frustrated and angry

*about it. Next time I would like you to say, even
briefly, what is upsetting you."*

It is often easier to tell other people what one "thinks" about something rather than what one "feels". Feelings are shown reluctantly or as a last resort at work. People need to feel able to say what they feel, particularly if it is negative. Otherwise feelings may erupt, people become angry and the situation gets out of control. It is equally useful for people who tend to engage in hot or cold conflict.

Negative feelings assertion has four separate parts. The first describes the behaviour which causes your feelings; the second describes the effect this has on you; the third describes the feelings it arouses; and the fourth describes the action you would like taken. It is important to mention your feelings later in your sentence. Expressed too early, your feelings stimulate the feelings of others.

Consequence assertion

Consequence assertion involves pointing out to the other person the potential consequences of their behaviour in a clear and unthreatening way. Examples of such statements are:

*"Unless you are able to hold open discussions with all
the parties concerned, I see no choice but to raise the
issues in a management meeting and I don't really
want to move things into a formal arena."*

*"If you continue to ignore our equal opportunities
policy I see no alternative but to start an internal
review and I don't want it to come to that."*

"If you persist in making unpleasant personal comments I will then start an official grievance procedure. I'd very much prefer to sort this between ourselves."

Consequence assertion is the most potent form of assertion and so should be used with care. Sometimes every other form of assertion may have been used and ignored and you still need to get your message across to the other person. There are three rules when using consequence assertion:

1. You have already tried other forms of assertiveness, which have not, so far, achieved their aim.

2. You have real sanctions that you genuinely mean to apply unless there is a change in behaviour or action.

3. There is a real alternative outcome if the person concerned does listen to and act on your message.

The style, method and tone of delivery of this kind of assertiveness is just as important as the words themselves. You are using this type of assertion to make it clear what the real consequences are for them, not to deliver a veiled threat.

FOGGING

When someone is behaving aggressively they tend to expect disagreement and charge ahead, not listening. Fogging is used to slow them down by an unexpected response. It is a way of side-stepping their issue and still retaining your point of view and integrity by agreeing with some part of what they say.

"Fogging" is so described because the effect is like suddenly facing fog when the way ahead appeared to be clear. As when someone is driving a car, this slows the person down sufficiently to hold them back and make them pay attention to what is behind the fog.

The word "Yes" can be a surprise and may help to "put the brakes on". For example, if someone said, "Well, that was a pretty stupid way to behave in a meeting", a "fogging" response might be, "Yes, I can see that you think that it was a pretty stupid way to behave." You are not agreeing that you have behaved stupidly, only that you can see that they believe that. Fogging gives time to reduce the temperature in a potentially explosive situation. Examples are:

Newly redundant manager: "I can't believe it, this company has let me down, they won't be able to manage without me!"

Personnel manager (fogging): "Yes, I know it must be a shock and that you feel that the company has let you down. You do have valuable knowledge and experience. Let's look at the possibilities that would be best for all."

Doctor: "You managers are a waste of space. Using all that stupid jargon and squandering money that could be better spent on patients."

Manager (fogging): "Yes, I know that jargon is frustrating, I've had my own difficulties getting used to medical terms and I agree that as much money as possible should be spent on patient care. That is why I want to discuss better ways of rostering staff."

INNER DIALOGUE

If you have a difficult meeting on your agenda an "inner conversation" might go like this:

"It's Friday … the budget meeting is today … it's a difficult meeting at the best of times and today I'm going to have to ask for extra cash … it won't go down well … they'll tell me I didn't do my forward planning well … it's not my fault I didn't know what would happen to prices … they won't accept that … this is just the chance Admin have been waiting for … now they'll have a go at me about costs in general … I know I won't get the extra money … I wish I was off ill today (or, I'm bound to lose my temper)."

All of this, of course, is negative, and these downward spiralling thoughts leave little room for assertive behaviour.

The sports world has discovered how to use inner dialogue to develop a positive approach in players. Positive inner dialogue is useful before a crisis or tricky situation to prepare yourself to do your best. It is not a question of pretending everything will be fine. It is a way of stopping the downward spiral with positive but realistic options. For example:

*"It's Friday ... the budget meeting is today ... it is
not going to be an easy meeting as I am going to ask
for extra money ... I do have a good case and I can
demonstrate that it is valid ... not everyone will be
helpful ... if there is any game played I do my best to
see my department has a fair hearing ... now, what
else is happening today?"*

An important aspect of positive inner dialogue is the
ability to move on to the next thing rather than remain
trapped in a difficult situation.

**Consider the opportunities for the use of the
above techniques in your conflict. Turn now to:**

BEHAVIOUR ANALYSIS

According to research into effective communicators
carried out by Neil Rackham and the Huthwaite
Research Group, the different behaviours discussed here
are useful and helpful.

Open behaviour

In making a statement about your feelings, you may have
to recognise your own role in creating these feelings.
Open behaviour reveals your own attitudes. They are
difficult to express positively if they are seen as hostile to

others. Feelings should be expressed about non-personal matters such as the quality of the relationship.

Seeking information

This involves asking questions, checking assumptions, and finding and exploring common ground. It is often more acceptable than direct disagreement. Such questions can often be used also to gain a breathing space when pressure and tension are mounting. Examples of such behaviour include: "What data support this proposal?" "Can you tell me what page this is on?" "Have these facts been checked?"

Building

This behaviour is particularly useful in showing how things may be made to work better in practice. When someone makes a suggestion there are usually some good points in it, and some weaknesses. Building behaviour directed to overcoming these weaknesses is called "patching". Examples include, "If I can take that further …" and "It will work better if …".

Supporting

Supporting behaviours often have most impact if the other person is not expecting them. In supporting an idea or suggestion, you also show support for the person. Supporting "noises" can be made, or specific statements such as, "Yes, I go along with that", "Sounds OK to me" and "I agree".

Bringing in

Bringing people into the conversation who have hitherto been unwilling or unable to make a contribution shows interest in them. It also indicates that their contribution is needed for the benefit of the whole. Examples can include, "Jack, I would like you to add your views", "Jo has been quiet - I wonder if she has anything to say", and "Bill, we really need your views".

Testing understanding

This behaviour puts the person asking for understanding in control of the discussion. It also helps agreements to be reached which can be implemented. Testing understanding helps clear up any ambiguities and probes possible areas of misunderstanding and confusion. Examples can include, "Can I just check whether we are talking about the same thing here?" and "Can I take it we all now agree?"

Summarising

Summarising makes clear and visible what any agreement (or disagreement) involves, and what people want to happen as a result. Examples include: "Looking back it looks as if we have decided (a) to accept the offer; (b) to implement the arrangement before the end of the year; and (c) to put Sue in charge."

Labelling

Any useful behaviour mentioned above is likely to have most positive impact if it is clearly indicted what is being said and what is the motive behind saying it. This is known as labelling or flagging. Everyone will find their own way and form of labelling, such as "Can I ask a question for clarification?" "In support of …".

Behaviour to avoid and discourage

Huthwaite's research discovered certain kinds of unhelpful verbal behaviour. These behaviours do not promote communication and often lead to a heightening of tension and eventual conflict.

Defend/attack spirals

Statements which are experienced as an attack by another party invariably bring out a defensive response and thereby start a spiral of increasing intensity. Any resultant defence against an attack is itself perceived as an attack by the other party. This then enables the other party to be blamed for causing the problem and both parties feel absolved of any responsibility.

Irritators

This behaviour often seems innocuous, yet has a very negative impact. It is often the prelude to a full-blown defend/attack spiral. Irritators "wind up" the other party. Very often particular individuals, working groups, professions and organizations develop their own forms of irritators. Examples include, "Our generous offer", "The reasonable case we are presenting", "We have done our homework" and "With the greatest respect".

Disagreement

Although disagreement is often about issues or facts, people experience the disagreement as personal. The sequencing of disagreement is important. If reasons for the disagreement are offered first then the disagreement itself may be more acceptable. If the statement of disagreement comes first then the reasons given will not be heard - the party is still smarting from the disagreement.

Argument dilution

Amassing reasons and mountains of information are not necessarily persuasive. They often do not tip the balance; instead, they only serve to confuse and create opportunities to expose and concentrate on weaknesses in the other's argument.

Shutting out

This is behaviour designed to exclude others or reduce their opportunity to contribute, and making them aware of what has been done. Interrupting others' flow of conversation can be done subtly or brutally - the effect is often the same.

Non-verbal behaviour

There are many ways a person can disrupt the conversation and "put others down" by altering their facial expression, posture or indirect comments. These can include:

- Showing clearly you are not listening - turning away
- Screwing up your face to show disapproval
- Finger pointing
- Talking over people
- Finishing off other people's sentences
- Sarcastic remarks.

Appendix:
Other Perspectives

Other models to contribute to an overall understanding of human behaviour. Their inclusion is designed to enrich the reader's insight, enhancing but not replacing the structured approach set out in the main text.

Contents

Appendix:
Other Perspectives

The perspectives and approaches presented here are not mutually exclusive in application. Different elements of each can be applied to a particular conflict.

TRANSACTIONAL ANALYSIS

First developed by Eric Berne, transactional analysis is a method of understanding different ways of being we all fall into at times, sometimes in repetitive patterns. (See his seminal book, *The Games People Play*, and Thomas A. Harris's *I'm OK - You're OK*). Berne identifies three main states: Parent, Adult and Child. These main states are not given their everyday meanings. In transactional analysis they take on different definitions. Your development according to this theory takes place in three main states and at two stages of your life: from birth to age five (Parent and Child), and from ten months onwards (Adult).

The Parent is your taught concept of life; it is what the people around you (at this stage it is mainly a person's parents, hence the term Parent) "inflict" on you until age five – the "don't do that!" and "do this!". This development can be both positive and negative. This affects how you develop, in that other people's (and especially the parents') foibles either become a part of your behaviour patterns and attitudes, or you behave in contrast to them. This could apply to any form of behaviour: how your mother, for example, drummed into your head that you must always wash your hands after going to the toilet because not to do so is dirty. So whenever you are in a position – even as an adult – where you cannot wash your hands through no fault of your own (because there is no soap and water available), you feel you are dirty, and you are not happy until you are able to wash them.

The Child is formed by what you have experienced yourself up to age five. It is how you as a child learn to respond to what you hear and see, and develops mainly as a direct result of the Parent experiences. This affects how you behave and again can be positive or negative. Therefore, using the above example, the fact you feel dirty because you have not washed your hands is your Child response: perhaps your mother severely reprimanded you as a toddler for not washing your hands and so you associate this action as "bad".

The Adult begins to develop at ten months. This is you as a thinking, feeling, separate being, when you begin to assess for yourself what is right and wrong, and how you feel towards things and other people (including your parents and siblings). You develop the ability to choose. This development continues for the rest of your life. In the above example, your Adult says: "There is no soap and water, so I cannot wash my hands. It is not my fault. Besides, the risk of my starting an epidemic because I cannot wash my hands just this once is exceptionally small." The Adult is, therefore, your voice of reason.

Berne examined these actions between people, words and behaviour and labelled them Transactions. In analysing these transactions he shows how an approach in one state triggers a response in another.

Parent

As a child you may have experienced Nurturing Parent behaviour. Some typical examples of Nurturing Parent behaviour towards a child might be:

"You'd better put a coat on because it's cold outside."

"I've packed you an extra cake in case you get hungry."

"Let me do that it's too hard for you."

However as Berne discovered, you don't have to be a parent to use these kinds of statements. Grown-ups use them all the time with each other. For example:

Worker to colleague: "Go home and lie down if you've got a temperature - I'll tell the boss so you won't get into trouble."

Secretary to manager: "I knew you'd forget your papers for the meeting so I did you an extra set this morning."

Line manager to junior: "I don't think you're really ready for a more difficult job yet."

The manner and tone of voice all play a part in delivering a Nurturing Parent statement. In most offices there is someone who remembers all the birthdays, does all the collections, looks out for vulnerable staff and endeavours to steer them away from difficulties. This is sometimes labelled as "mothering" behaviour. Most people, however, on some occasions or within particular relationships, behave like this even if it is only occasional. Some words that typify this state are Caring, Interpreting, Protecting, Guiding, Shielding, Supporting, Filtering, Pampering, and Comforting.

The second type of parent state is that of Critical or Controlling Parent. Again, as children, most people have had some experience of a grown-up, parent or teacher, who monitored and evaluated their behaviour for mistakes and transgressions - someone who has power over what you can do or have, and expresses it in a negative and critical way. Some examples of Critical/ Controlling Parent behaviour towards a child might be:

"No, you can't stay out after eight, because I say so, that's why."

"Your bedroom is a mess, tidy it up now."

"What do you think you look like? Change those clothes immediately, I have to live with the neighbours."

"I've told you three times not to do that and I don't want to tell you again!"

"What time do you call this?"

Once again you don't have to be a parent to use these kind of statements. For example:

Boss to worker: "Your must tidy your desk."

Colleague to colleague: "What time do you call this?"

Manager to junior: "This needs a lot of work to improve it."

Senior to junior: "No you can't go to the conference."

The manner and tone of delivery are important, as is the body language. In most workplaces there is someone everyone wants to avoid because their way of managing is critical parenting behaviour. They will always find the flaw, nothing will ever be good enough and very little will be delegated as that may be seen as a loss of personal power. They are sometimes labelled as "Dictators" or "Dragons". Everyone has some element of this state of being and occasionally conflicts will bring this to the fore. Some words that typify critical or controlling parent behaviour are Preventing, Judging, Undermining, Chastising, Overbearing, Dominating, and Directing.

Child

Berne identifies two child states. The first, Free or Natural Child describes your earliest behaviour. Before you learn the rules that govern families and society you were in a Free or Natural state. You make direct and honest statements because you haven't been taught to be different. Free or natural child statements might be:

"I won't kiss Grandma - she has hairs on her chin."

"Why is that man so tall?"

"I want a biscuit" or "I want it all."

"I don't want to go to bed, I'm not sleepy."

"Why do you paint your face?"

By the time a child has learned to talk, some of their free spirit has been curtailed, often by Critical and Controlling Parent transactions (see above). The natural curiosity and exuberance of childhood is moulded and shaped by Nurturing Parent behaviour (otherwise children could come to harm) and by Critical and Controlling Parent behaviour (so that they learn to adapt and fit in to society). Most people still have a bit of Free Child within them, which is most in evidence at play or leisure, but is sometimes manifested in anger and conflict. In many workplaces there is at least one person who breaks the rules, makes fun of everything, and is always ready for a joke - a kind of jester who lightens the atmosphere but can occasionally go too far. Some words that typify free or natural child behaviours are Carefree, Open, Lively, Instinctive, Confident, Spontaneous, Impulsive and Unprompted.

The second child state is that of Adapted Child. This is where the Free or Natural Child state has been shaped and moulded to meet society's habits. Thus you do things to be liked, to get noticed, and to get your own way. You adapt to being nurtured and so sometimes feel unable to tackle things by yourself. You feel nervous about failure or anger, and so live within safe limits and boundaries set by others. You may also adapt your behaviour to cope with Critical and Controlling Parent behaviour and the unequal balance of power. Typical Adapted Child responses might be:

"It's not fair!"

"I can't, I won't, why do I have to?"

"Why is it always me that has to do the dishes?"

"It's not my fault, they made me."

The switch from trying to be liked and being given things to temper tantrums or sulking can be swift. Yet they are all adaptations to cope with the actions and behaviours used in transacting with others. Once again these same statements can be heard in any workplace.

Worker to colleague: "It's not fair."

Worker to supervisor: "Why is it always me who has to work late?"

Boss to secretary: "I want the work done now."

Worker to supervisor: "I couldn't go to the meeting on my own, couldn't someone come with me?"

Supervisor to boss: "I'm ever so sorry to bother you, but would it be all right if I had Thursday off for a doctor's appointment?"

Some words that typify Adapted Child behaviour are Sulking, Attention seeking, Temper tantrums, Under-confident, Dependent, Approval seeking, Aggressive, Passive, Pouting, and Moody.

★

Everyone has the ability to transact and respond in all these modes. So what is it in conflict situations which triggers a particular response in each of us? Someone may have a point of view that you might think perfectly reasonable, but if they deliver it out of the Critical or Controlling Parent mode, this immediately triggers an Adapted Child response from you and a conflict is created.

Think about the conflict situation you identified earlier and consider the range of transactions and modes of being. When looking for ways to change behaviour a good place to start is with transactional analysis moving into adult behaviour and encouraging it from others.

PROJECTION

The process of blaming and regarding someone else as responsible for your weaknesses is called Projection by psychologists. An examination of projection may give vital clues about the reasons for behaviour patterns that exist in your living case example which have no other logical explanation.

In a conflict parties become weaker (as they come under increasing attack). They are often unable to face up to their own weaknesses and project them onto others. They then blame others for these weaknesses and proceed to attack them.

Projection results in blaming other people, the circumstances and the environment – in other words, looking for scapegoats. This results in more frustration as the parties each suppress their own feelings. But they are dimly aware of their own shortcomings and become increasingly angry with themselves. By "exporting" these feelings to others, others are used as a screen on which feelings and fears can be projected. Each party can justify their accusations. Nobody is perfect, especially as the conflict brings out the worst in everyone. Frustration also builds up in the other party, the object of the projection. Being accused of inventions or exaggerations makes one feel trapped.

THE DRAMA TRIANGLE

Relationships in conflicts often start by each party taking up one of three roles:

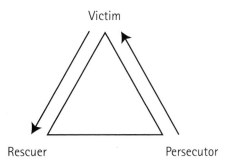

The Victim feels badly treated by the Persecutor but does not deal with this directly. Instead the Victim seeks out a sympathetic Rescuer and tells them enough of the story to gain sympathy and support. This solace can feel so good that the Victim continues to bring stories and snippets of information, maybe even sharing these with additional rescuers. If this continues the Rescuer begins to feel like a Victim.

So many people now have such a one-sided view of events that they feel badly dealt with and may begin to seek their own Rescuers. In the meantime the Rescuer has become the repository of the aggrieved stories of the Victim for so long they begin to feel trapped and dread the latest version or news of the most recent slights, and so feel that they have become a Victim and are being Persecuted. In this way the roles change in a game of triangular musical chairs. This situation is made even worse if the Rescuer actually intervenes. The Victim becomes more powerless in their own and other people's minds. The Rescuer may also have turned themselves into a legitimate target for attack by their intervention.

The key to breaking this endless activity is the Rescuer. When first approached they should be empathetically assertive rather than sympathetic. For example:

> *Don't say:"Oh dear, that sounds awful, I'm not surprised you are so upset. I would be too, they shouldn't be allowed to get away with it."*

> *Do say:"I can see you're upset, and from what you have said I can see why. How can I help you to go and sort it out."*

By refusing to rescue and be a depository (i.e. a mere safe haven) of the hurt and anxiety, the onus remains with the Victim to manage the situation. The removal of the Rescuer role prevents the escalation of the conflict and the expansion of the number of participants.

THE DOUBLE – THE ANGEL AND THE SHADOW

The shadow is what a person is on a bad day. It is the behaviour a person is sorry about and ashamed of, even though it may not be typical, but at the time seemed impossible to avoid. The angel is also an illusion based on a person's ideal self-image. The angel is represented by those things a person is able to do well, what a person is on a good day. It is their potential and possibilities. It is the behaviour and achievements they are proud of.

The pattern of always anticipating negative responses or behaviour from the other party can be broken by:

- Taming, not fighting the double.
- Facing up to the double by confronting and picturing it.
- Redeeming the double.
- Thinking of golden moments in the relationship through the working of the angel.

THE DOUBLE BIND

The double bind is a common psychological mechanism in families and marriages that are not working well. It is a negative contract between people that prescribes and expects certain behaviour. As a result both parties ascribe negative roles to the other. It is commonly known as a "love-hate" relationship.

Parties fight against each other in a conflict but paradoxically they need each other. This results in a whole sequence of self-fulfilling prophecies. So each party meets its own double and shadow through the double or shadow of the other. In hierarchically structured organizations there are ample opportunities for dominant - submissive, master - servant type binds to become established. For example, the dominant manager says: "If only they would take more initiative". The submissive employee says: "If only they would give me more space". Double binds are often characterised by phrases such as:

"Please give me another chance."

"Just be normal like everyone else."

"In the end it all comes down to me."

"You must help me to be/do better."

Roles once fixed are difficult if not impossible to unfix. The parties increasingly need and rely on each other through the double bind. However, even though the bind may be a negative one, it is better than no relationship at all.

PERSONAL APPROACHES TO CONFLICT

Professor John Gottman of Washington State University has carried out research into successful partnerships. He identified three different approaches to conflict.

The *volatile conflict embracer* is someone that relishes an argument; is sensitive to criticism; blows up and lets off steam; has instant negative reactions; moves away from the conflict immediately it is finished.

The *contained conflict avoider*, in contrast, hates a row; overlooks problems and denies difference; swallows slights and insults; will put up with anything to avoid trouble.

The third approach is taken by the *aware conflict validator* who checks the seriousness of potential difficulty; has a measured response; listens carefully to other views; puts things in perspective; doesn't back away from important issues.

Clearly if partnerships are in matched pairs there will be few difficulties. Two conflict embracers will have many rows and fights, but get over them very quickly. Two conflict avoiders will tip-toe around any dissension and accommodate each other in a careful way. Two conflict validators will check and validate situations and feelings, dealing firmly with issues as they arise. The problems arise when these roles become mixed and behave in ways that frustrate, hurt or irritate the other.

Four philosophies of the concept of conflict

Fundamentally different concepts as to the essence and function of conflict can hinder mutual understanding and the overcoming of differences. This is because one party may hope for a real breakthrough in the development of a particular situation by a forceful confrontation, and prepare to play a very active part in it, whilst another party sees the conflict as a struggle of fundamental ideals and principles, in which the people in the conflict are merely players - pawns in a deadly game. The theories summarised here are based on Professor Fritz Glasl's and Bernard Livegoed's ideas about the philosophical stances taken by people when faced with questions and challenges.

Materialism

The determining factor in a conflict is the distribution of physical resources. Conflicts are therefore ways of redistributing power. All behaviour and psychological factors can be explained by reference to the underlying material struggle which is taking place. Conflicts are conducted according to the rules of game theories and rational strategies.

Spiritualism

This view of the real purpose of conflicts is different to materialism. Here, conflicts are seen as the battleground for super-human powers. These confrontations and struggles take place against a background of promoting or impeding progress. In conflicts the players are constantly called upon to assess where they stand in relation to the forces at work (e.g. good and evil act on this).

Realism

In this case, conflicts are seen as a rather unfortunate but necessary evil. They belong to life, like birth and death. A tendency towards aggressive behaviour in human beings will inevitably lead to conflict. For example, uncontrolled impulses and other personality factors may all play a role. You can do something about conflicts for they are open to better conditions, training and so on.

Idealism

Conflicts are seen here as the midwives of all social and other developments. With the help of conflict, outdated existing structures can be demolished, new principles can be established, and new forms found. Without conflicts there would be stagnation and no progress. The expression "you can't make an omelette without cracking eggs" is a good analogy.

Activities

This part contains the Activities mentioned throughout the book. The aim is for you to carry out these Activities so that you can create your own living case study conflict, which should be based on a current conflict you are having to deal with, or a past conflict that you can revisit and assess whether you could have done things differently to achieve a more satisfactory result. To gain the most from these Activities, carry them out as you are reading the book; in this way, you can refer back to your results as the conflict resolution techniques described in this book progress.

Each Activity begins with an explanation of how to carry out the exercise followed by the Activity itself. There is space provided here for you to complete the Activities, but if you need more space you may find it easier to create your own living case study conflict journal.

Contents

Activity 1: Basic Questionnaire

Think about the conflict you have identified as your living case study and answer the following questions about it. At this stage do not think too deeply about the situation; you will be able to analyse things more later on, using various devices designed for the purpose. At this stage put down your first impressions and your immediate thoughts.

1. How would you describe the conflict? Can you give it a name or a simple description?

2. What did the conflict appear to be about when it started?

3. Over time did the reasons for the conflict shift or change?

From Fritchie R and Leary M (1998) *Resolving Conflicts in Organizations*, Lemos & Crane, London

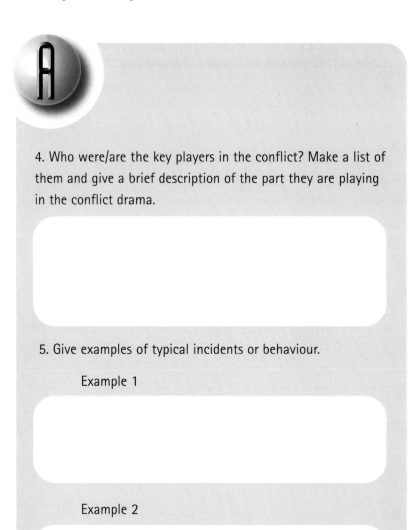

4. Who were/are the key players in the conflict? Make a list of them and give a brief description of the part they are playing in the conflict drama.

5. Give examples of typical incidents or behaviour.

Example 1

Example 2

Example 3

From Fritchie R and Leary M (1998) *Resolving Conflicts in Organizations*, Lemos & Crane, London

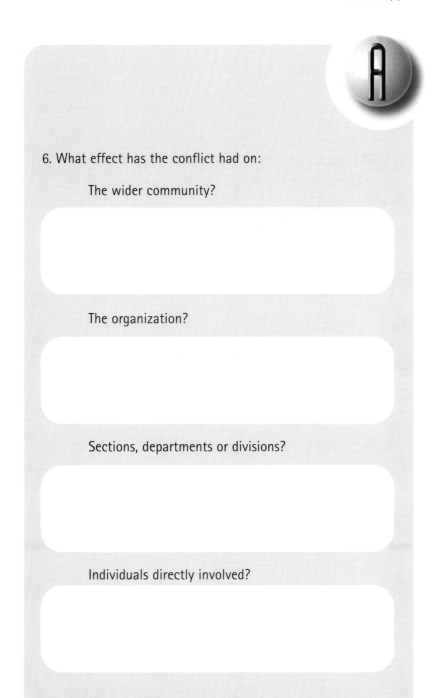

6. What effect has the conflict had on:

The wider community?

The organization?

Sections, departments or divisions?

Individuals directly involved?

Individuals indirectly involved?

7. Where did the conflict end up or where is it now?

From Fritchie R and Leary M (1998) *Resolving Conflicts in Organizations*, Lemos & Crane, London

Activity 2: Hot and Cold Conflict Questionnaire

This Activity concentrates on the general climate (hot or cold) conditions of your living case study. Read the statements and give each of them a rating score of 1 to 5 on the following basis:
Score 1. This does not happen at all, at any time.
Score 2. This happens a little, some of the time.
Score 3. It is somewhat like this.
Score 4. It is like this most of the time.
Score 5. It is very much like this, all of the time.

Statement	*Score*
1. There is a great deal of enthusiasm, commitment and determination to achieve objectives.	☐
2. People are very cynical: no-one seems particularly bothered about what happens.	☐
3. No-one seems to know what they are doing or care about the effects on other people.	☐
4. The parties do not seem to be working towards any ideals or aims.	☐
5. There is often a great deal more heat than light.	☐
6. It's difficult to know what is really going on - it's all behind closed doors.	☐

From Fritchie R and Leary M (1998) *Resolving Conflicts in Organizations*, Lemos & Crane, London

Statement	Score
7. People make threats and try to bully each other.	☐
8. There are strong reactions to what is said and done, nothing goes unnoticed.	☐
9. Most of the time nothing seems to be happening at all	☐
10. Action seems to be taken for the sake of doing something, but no one seems to care.	☐
11. People pretend that the conflict is not affecting them in any way.	☐
12. People lay traps for each other and try to catch each other out.	☐
13. The parties all seem to have high opinions of themselves.	☐
14. People seem to have a lot of energy and stamina.	☐
15. Everyone seems to have a very low opinion of themselves.	☐

From Fritchie R and Leary M (1998) *Resolving Conflicts in Organizations*, Lemos & Crane, London

A

Statement	Score
16. People tend to seek each other out, and go for each other when they meet.	☐
17. People seem embarrassed and tense when they meet each other.	☐
18. There is a lethargic, tired atmosphere around people.	☐
19. Everyone seems to be joining in the conflict and having a good time.	☐
20. People seem to be purposely avoiding each other.	☐
21. The parties are very busy fighting their cause going all out to win.	☐
22. There is a lot of noise and frantic activity around.	☐

From Fritchie R and Leary M (1998) *Resolving Conflicts in Organizations*, Lemos & Crane, London

Now transfer your scores for each statement onto the scoring grid below:

STATEMENT	SCORE	STATEMENT	SCORE
1.	☐	2.	☐
5.	☐	3.	☐
7.	☐	4.	☐
8.	☐	6.	☐
10.	☐	9.	☐
13.	☐	11.	☐
14.	☐	12.	☐
16.	☐	15.	☐
19.	☐	17.	☐
21.	☐	18.	☐
22.	☐	20.	☐
TOTAL Column A	☐	TOTAL Column B	☐

From Fritchie R and Leary M (1998) *Resolving Conflicts in Organizations*, Lemos & Crane, London

Interpreting your scores

Column A
A score of between 40 and 55 indicates your conflict is extremely hot and and is in danger of becoming explosive. The circumstances need cooling down quickly. A score of less than 20 means there is very little hot conflict around.

Column B
A score of between 40 and 55 indicates your conflict is extremely cold and is likely to result in damage through its insidious nature. The situation needs warming up quickly. A score of less than 20 means there is very little cold conflict around.

Columns A and B
A score of more than 40 in both columns indicates that there is a great deal of hot and cold conflict around; you should look closely at which parties are hot and which are cold. A score of below 20 in both columns means there is very little of any conflict around at all; in this case it may be useful to look again at the Column B statements to check that there are no cold conflicts that have not yet surfaced.

From Fritchie R and Leary M (1998) *Resolving Conflicts in Organizations,*
Lemos & Crane, London

Activity 3: Hot or Cold Personal Preferences

Complete the following questionnaire and using the rating scale provided calculate your hot and cold personal preference score.
Score 1. Not at all, anytime.
Score 2. A little, sometimes.
Score 3. Somewhat.
Score 4. Like this most of the time.
Score 5. Very much like this all the time.

Statement	*Score*
1. I get enthusiastic, committed and determined to achieve objectives.	5
2. I am cynical and not really bothered about what happens.	2
3. I don't care about the effects of what is done to other people.	1
4. I am not working towards any particular aims or ideals.	1
5. I tend to generate more heat than light.	1
6. I do things behind closed doors, so no-one else knows what is going on.	1

From Fritchie R and Leary M (1998) *Resolving Conflicts in Organizations*, Lemos & Crane, London

A

7. I make threats and try to bully others. | 1 |

8. I react strongly to what is said and done –
nothing goes unnoticed. | 3 |

9. I give the impression that nothing
much is happening at all. | 3 |

10. I take action for the sake of doing something. | 1 |

11. I pretend that the conflict is not
affecting me in any way. | 1 |

12. I lay traps for other people
and try to catch them out. | 1 |

13. I have a pretty high opinion of myself
and what I am doing. | 4 |

14. I work up lots of energy and stamina. | 3 |

15. I have a pretty low opinion of myself
and what I am doing. | 1 |

16. I seek other people out, tell them
what I think and go for them if necessary. | 4 |

From Fritchie R and Leary M (1998) *Resolving Conflicts in Organizations*, Lemos & Crane, London

17. I feel embarrassed and tense when I meet others. `2`

18. I feel lethargic and tired about it all. `1`

19. I like to join in the conflict
    and have a good time. `1`

20. I avoid contact with other people if
    at all possible. `5`

21. I fight my cause as strongly as possible.
    I go all out to win. `4`

22. I add to the noise and general frantic activity. `1`

From Fritchie R and Leary M (1998) *Resolving Conflicts in Organizations*, Lemos & Crane, London

Now transfer your scores for each statement onto the scoring grid below:

STATEMENT	SCORE		STATEMENT	SCORE
1.	5		2.	2
5.	1		3.	1
7.	1		4.	1
8.	3		6.	1
10.	1		9.	3
13.	4		11.	1
14.	3		12.	1
16.	4		15.	1
19.	1		17.	2
21.	4		18.	1
22.	1		20.	5
TOTAL Column A	28		TOTAL Column B	19

From Fritchie R and Leary M (1998) *Resolving Conflicts in Organizations*, Lemos & Crane, London

Interpreting your scores

Column A   A score of over 40 in this column indicates
                   you are extremely hot in conflicts. You
                   may need to cool down a little.

Column B   A score of over 40 in this column means
                   you are extremely cold in conflicts. You
                   may need to warm up a little.

Column A and B   A score of over 40 in both columns
                   indicates that you have no strong
                   preferences in how you behave in
                   conflicts, but your actual behaviour in
                   both ways is strong. People may feel that
                   your behaviour is not predictable and so
                   may not take your attempts to resolve the
                   conflict at all seriously. A score of below
                   20 in both columns, however, suggests
                   that you would prefer to avoid conflicts
                   altogether.

From Fritchie R and Leary M (1998) *Resolving Conflicts in Organizations*, Lemos & Crane, London

Activity 4: Temperaments Questionnaire

Think of yourself when dealing with conflicts. What tempera-ment (as we described in Chapter 3) are you likely to bring to the conflict and how will this affect the way you behave? The following questionnaire enables you to decide what your main temperament is. Once you have decided this, check back to Chapter 3: is this an accurate picture of how you behave in con-flict? If you are in any doubt, ask your friends and colleagues how they have experienced you.

Consider each statement included below and rate yourself using the following scale:
Score 1- Not at all like this, anytime.
Score 2 - A little like this, sometimes.
Score 3 - Somewhat like this.
Score 4 - Quite like this much of the time.
Score 5 - Very much like this all of the time.

Statement	*Score*
1. I have very strong opinions that I express forcefully.	
2. I try to conserve my energy and effort until it is really needed.	
3. I tend to feel rather self - conscious and nervous.	

From Fritchie R and Leary M (1998) *Resolving Conflicts in Organizations*, Lemos & Crane, London

4. I avoid trouble if I possibly can.

5. I like to have as much information as possible.

6. I say "Yes" or "No" to things; never "Maybe".

7. I either strongly identify with the issues
   and people involved, or not at all.

8. I seem to know more about the
   subject than the others.

9. I need time to digest things and think
   about what is going on.

10. I think on my feet, often whilst I am speaking.

11. I take time to make up my mind and
    decide what to do.

12. I don't like instant comments and reactions;
    it is best to think before speaking.

13. I like to know about people's motives.

From Fritchie R and Leary M (1998) *Resolving Conflicts in Organizations*, Lemos & Crane, London

A

14. I do not find it difficult to say "No"
    and confront problems.

15. I like to please people whenever I can.
    I don't like saying "No" or upsetting them.

16. I don't like surprises; I like to know
    exactly what is going on.

17. I need to be convinced by seeing for myself
    and I rely heavily on my own experiences.

18. I move into any situation quickly and
    try to make the maximum impact possible

19. I tend to jump to conclusions very
    quickly and have strong immediate impressions.

20. I tease people rather than confront
    them directly.

21. I don't like to receive any negative
    comments or criticism.

22. I tend to act as I see fit at the time.

23. I don't lose my patience easily -
    but when I do, watch out!

From Fritchie R and Leary M (1998) *Resolving Conflicts in Organizations*,
Lemos & Crane, London

24. I can change my mind very quickly
and I'm not always sure why.

☐

Now transfer your questionnaire scores for each statement onto the grid below.

Statement	Score	Statement	Score	Statement	Score	Statement	Score
1	☐	3	☐	4	☐	2	☐
6	☐	5	☐	10	☐	11	☐
7	☐	9	☐	15	☐	12	☐
8	☐	13	☐	19	☐	16	☐
14	☐	17	☐	22	☐	20	☐
18	☐	21	☐	24	☐	23	☐
Total	☐	Total	☐	Total	☐	Total	☐
Column A		Column B		Column C		Column D	

From Fritchie R and Leary M (1998) *Resolving Conflicts in Organizations*, Lemos & Crane, London

Interpreting your scores

A score of more than 20 indicates the following temperament:

- In column A, a strong CHOLERIC temperament.
- In column B, a strong MELANCHOLIC temperament.
- In column C, a strong SANGUINE temperament.
- In column D, a strong PHLEGMATIC temperament.

Now look at your next highest score: this may indicate your "back up" temperament. This back-up temperament will act to moderate anything you do and support the best efforts that result from your main temperament.

From Fritchie R and Leary M (1998) *Resolving Conflicts in Organizations*, Lemos & Crane, London

Activity 5: The Escalator Checklist

To ensure your subsequent conflict resolution efforts are productive, you can plot the level to which your conflict living case study has escalated using the Conflict Escalator framework.

Here a summary of the main features at each phase and level of escalation is provided to help you decide. With your living case example in mind, look at all nine levels described below. Which level most characterises your conflict at the moment? Highlight or underline the level you think it has reached.

The dynamics of conflict escalation means that there is always a tendency for the conflict to move on to the next level of seriousness. When you assess which level your living case study has reached on the Escalator, it may be that the conflict has first broken through from the level below and that new patterns of behaviour are only just being established. It could be that the conflict has been carried out at a particular level of intensity for sometime and certain behaviour has become the norm. It may also be that, although you have decided that the conflict is at a certain level, there are signs that the conflict is about to break through to the next level.

 From Fritchie R and Leary M (1998) *Resolving Conflicts in Organizations*, Lemos & Crane, London

Phase 1: Nervousness

Level 1: discussion

>   Minor misunderstandings and tensions interrupting
>   the process of dealing with issues in a rational way.

Level 2: debate

>   This results in the parties becoming more separated
>   and polarised; a solution is now further away.

Level 3: deeds not words

>   Trust begins to break down and words are not
>   enough.

Phase 2: Neurosis

Level 4: fixations

>   Stereotypical images are built up – confirmed by many
>   self-fulfilling prophecies. Psychological distance grows.
>   Coalitions and alliances are formed with supporters.

Level 5: loss of face

>   People's reputations and integrity are threatened and
>   individuals can be badly hurt.

Level 6: threats

>   Parties react in direct, specific ways by making and
>   carrying out threats resulting in the very action they
>   are seeking to prevent.

From Fritchie R and Leary M (1998) *Resolving Conflicts in Organizations*,
Lemos & Crane, London

Phase 3: pathology

Level 7: inhumanity

> All confrontations become tougher. The parties have little or no human dignity left in each other's eyes and can therefore be treated as an object.

Level 8: attack on nerves

> Destructive behaviour is now a goal in itself. The focus is on isolating the other party.

Level 9: no way back

> Ultimately each party sows the seeds of its own destruction.

From Fritchie R and Leary M (1998) *Resolving Conflicts in Organizations*, Lemos & Crane, London

Activity 6: Moments of Truth

This exercise offers you a different approach than Activity 6 to identifying the level of escalation in your living case study. Here you can short cut the process of identification by using cameo pictures or expressions.

You may be able to tell immediately which level of escalation has been reached; sometimes more detailed consideration may be needed. In the latter case, use the descriptions of each phase and level of escalation as a checklist against which to check what is happening in your living case example.

The "moments of truth" occur in a conflict when something is said or done which somehow sums up concisely and precisely what the conflict is all about and indicates clearly the stage to which it has escalated. The parties almost seem to collude with each other to make a shared statement or otherwise give a signal which says "right - this is it" or "this is what it is all about".

The following table gives some indication of the likely moment of truth statements which typify each level of escalation. It is a crude but often effective form of diagnosis.

Look through the "moments of truth" list and highlight or underline any statements which sum up the level of escalation in your living case study.

From Fritchie R and Leary M (1998) *Resolving Conflicts in Organizations*, Lemos & Crane, London

Escalation level	Moments of truth
Level 1: discussion Main issue: We have different positions.	"It's obvious you don't understand." "I fundamentally disagree." "You are wrong." "You cannot be serious!"
Level 2: debate Main issue: We have opposing positions.	"I don't care what you say, we're against it." "We will win the argument on this one."
Level 3: deeds not words Main issue: It's a question of trust.	"You have let us down too often." "How do we know you won't let us down?" "That's typical."
Level 4: fixations Main issue: There are now negative images.	"Everyone should know what you are really like." "We've lost all respect for them." "They are not nice people to deal with."

From Fritchie R and Leary M (1998) *Resolving Conflicts in Organizations*, Lemos & Crane, London

Escalation level	Moments of truth
Level 5: loss of face Main issue: It's a question of self-respect.	"We are better than they are." "There's no going back now." "Let me tell you what they have done now."
Level 6: strategies of threat Main issue: It's now damage limitation.	"We have no alternative but to... " "If you don't ...then we will be forced to... " "They must be stopped."
Level 7: inhumanity Main issue: It's a question of identity.	"They deserve all that they get." "They are not worth talking to." "The ends justify the means."
Level 8: attack on nerves Main Issue: How to get isolation.	"Nobody agrees with what they are doing." "They are completely out on a limb."
Level 9: No way back Main issue: Increase the others' loss.	"We will never give in."

From Fritchie R and Leary M (1998) *Resolving Conflicts in Organizations*,
Lemos & Crane, London

Activity 7: Escalation Questionnaire

This Activity will when completed give you the most detailed assessment of the level of conflict in your living case study. Examine each of the following statements and score them on a rating scale of 1 to 5, as follows:

Score 1 – The situation is not at all like this.
Score 2 – It is a bit like this, occasionally.
Score 3 – It is somewhat like this, some of the time.
Score 4 – It is rather like this, most of the time.
Score 5 – It is very much like this, all of the time.

Statement   *Score*

1. During the discussions people take up fixed positions. ☐

2. People defend the positions they have taken up. ☐

3. People try to persuade others to share their views and ideas. ☐

4. Parties become unco-operative and argumentative. ☐

5. The conversation gets stuck and progress is blocked. ☐

6. The parties start closing ranks. ☐

7. People begin to keep their distance. ☐

From Fritchie R and Leary M (1998) *Resolving Conflicts in Organizations*, Lemos & Crane, London

8. Listening is reduced and people become
   most concerned with their own arguments. ☐

9. People only hear what they would
   like to hear and ignore the rest. ☐

10. The argument gets a little heated at times. ☐

11. Frustration begins to set in –
    we want to get on but others won't let us. ☐

12. Each party thinks its arguments are the
    strongest and therefore will prevail in the end. ☐

13. Everyone struggles to show that they
    are equal or superior to the others. ☐

14. Thinking becomes polarised. ☐

15. There seems to be little common
    ground or interest. ☐

16. People use unfair verbal tricks and tactics. ☐

17. People are very careful about what
    they say and how they say it. ☐

From Fritchie R and Leary M (1998) *Resolving Conflicts in Organizations*, Lemos & Crane, London

18. Positions and views are seen as irreconcilable. ☐

19. People are more concerned to impress others rather than listen to others' arguments. ☐

20. There is a competition going on based on logical reasoning. ☐

21. People seem to be more concerned with actions than words. ☐

22. The parties stop talking to each other, convinced they will get nowhere. ☐

23. Positions are fixed - only actions will change things now, not talking about them. ☐

24. Parties rehearse what they will do to put into practice what they have been arguing. ☐

25. Non-verbal signs and signals are picked up and discussed – privately. ☐

From Fritchie R and Leary M (1998) *Resolving Conflicts in Organizations*, Lemos & Crane, London

26. Any discrepancies between what people say and what they do are pounced upon. ☐

27. Negative attitudes and intentions enter the conversation. ☐

28. Trust has become an issue. ☐

29. The parties begin to close ranks and insist everyone on their side conforms. ☐

30. Strong leaders emerge to become spokespersons for the rest of the group. ☐

31. Its now a question of who will win and who will lose. ☐

32. Images have become fixed and each side sees itself in a better light than the others. ☐

33. Point scoring games are carried out on an intellectual, professional or occupational basis. ☐

34. Communication becomes repetitive and predictable. ☐

35. Parties begin to appeal to others to support their case. ☐

From Fritchie R and Leary M (1998) *Resolving Conflicts in Organizations*, Lemos & Crane, London

36. Campaigns to gain sympathy and
    support are organized. ☐

37. Coalitions of different parties are
    formed with those who are on the same side. ☐

38. Images and views become more extreme -
    positive in the case of each side and
    negative in its group view of the other. ☐

39. The parties only see what they want to
    see and hear what they want to hear. ☐

40. Each party feels that only it (and its supporters)
    understand its position. ☐

41. Parties start to attack each other's reputation. ☐

42. Each party tries to prove the others are
    untrustworthy, unreliable or misleading. ☐

43. The basic integrity of each party is questioned. ☐

44. People feel let down, disappointed and disillusioned. ☐

45. Rituals of punishment and banishment are
    carried out against everyone who opposes. ☐

From Fritchie R and Leary M (1998) *Resolving Conflicts in Organizations*, Lemos & Crane, London

46. People feel isolated, cut off and "bad"
about themselves. ☐

47. There is a struggle to boost self-image
and re-establish some dignity. ☐

48. Each party's concepts and views of itself and
the others change radically and for the worse. ☐

49. Behaviour becomes rigid and strict,
particularly towards the "enemy". ☐

50. Every minor issue becomes a battle
between right ("us") and wrong ("them"). ☐

51. The level of violence (verbal and non-verbal)
and aggression has increased. ☐

52. The degeneration of the conflict has increased,
things are now out of control . ☐

53. The use of threats becomes more predominant
and dominates the conversation. ☐

54. Attempts are made to change the others'
position (and mind) by exerting pressure. ☐

From Fritchie R and Leary M (1998) *Resolving Conflicts in Organizations*,
Lemos & Crane, London

55. Threats towards the other party are answered with counter-threats.

56. Minor threats are carried out to show the others that "we mean what we say".

57. Defensiveness increases, which then becomes aggressive, preventative action.

58. Each party plans to meet the worst of all possibilities; it hears the worst and plans for it to happen.

59. Crisis decision-making patterns are emerging.

60. Each party feels "under siege" but may also make preventative "strikes" at the enemy.

61. Systematic destructive campaigns against the sanctions potential of the other party are carried out.

62. The deliberate intention to cause damage to each other becomes dominant.

63. It is no longer possible to achieve anything positive.

From Fritchie R and Leary M (1998) *Resolving Conflicts in Organizations*, Lemos & Crane, London

64. Each party's concern for damaging the
    other is greater than concern for damaging itself.

65. The target of each attack is to undermine
    the position of the other party.

66. One party's aims are to paralyse the other
    party, to stop it at all costs.

67. The other party is totally discredited. It deserves it.

68. Seeing the weaknesses of the other side is
    compensation for any loss a party may incur.

69. The ends justify the means.

70. The other party must be exposed for
    what it really is.

71. Each party's aim is to isolate the other side
    and cut it off from all means of support.

72. Each party tries to influence others to act
    against the other party.

73. Rumours are spread and scandals exposed.

From Fritchie R and Leary M (1998) *Resolving Conflicts in Organizations*,
Lemos & Crane, London

74. Each party's actions are directed at cutting off the other party's means of retreat, making withdrawal impossible. ☐

75. There is no going back now - for anyone. ☐

76. Behaviour has become completely irrational – except in terms of conflict itself. ☐

77. Going ahead with the conflict and continuing is preferable to withdrawal and capitulation. ☐

78. Each party is prepared to do what is necessary to "beat" the other side no matter what the cost. ☐

79. Parties are prepared to risk more damage to themselves, as long as the other side suffers. ☐

80. There is no calculation of the costs and potential benefits of any action. ☐

81. There are no limits to acts of violence. ☐

82. Things are completely out of control, everyone seems powerless to do anything. ☐

From Fritchie R and Leary M (1998) *Resolving Conflicts in Organizations*, Lemos & Crane, London

83. The conflict has to end with the complete
negation and destruction of the other side.

84. Direct confrontation with the enemy
is the only option.

85. All the buttons of destruction are pushed
at once - it's all or nothing.

86. Everyone in the environment is involved in the
conflict - no-one is allowed to remain neutral.

87. Each party's own destruction is acceptable
- as long as the other side is destroyed as well.

88. To continue the fight to the end is the only choice.

89. There is a complete domination of
destructive goals and aims

90. There is a feeling of inevitability about the
situation; there is no way out and all is lost

*Now transfer your scores for each statement onto the following
scoring grid and total up each column Levels 1 - 9.*

From Fritchie R and Leary M (1998) *Resolving Conflicts in Organizations*,
Lemos & Crane, London

Level 1		Level 2		Level 3		Level 4		Level 5		Level 6		Level 7		Level 8		Level 9	
Statement	Score	Statement	Score	Statement	Score	Statement	Score	Statement	Score	Statement	Score	Statement	Score	Statement	Score	Statement	Score
1		11		21		31		41		51		61		71		81	
2		12		22		32		42		52		62		72		82	
3		13		23		33		43		53		63		73		83	
4		14		24		34		44		54		64		74		84	
5		15		25		35		45		55		65		75		85	
6		16		26		36		46		56		66		76		86	
7		17		27		37		47		57		67		77		87	
8		18		28		38		48		58		68		78		88	
9		19		29		39		49		59		69		79		89	
10		20		30		40		50		60		70		80		90	

Totals

From Fritchie R and Leary M (1998) *Resolving Conflicts in Organizations*, Lemos & Crane, London

Interpreting your scores

Now look at the totals at the foot of the score grid. The column with highest score indicates the level your living case study conflict has reached on the Conflict Escalator. The higher score – of 35 or more – the stronger the indication. Where there are two high scores of over 35, there is a strong possibility that the conflict is breaking through to a higher level. For example, a score of 42 in Level 3 and a score of 38 in Level 4 means that the conflict is moving into Level 4 of conflict escalation.

From Fritchie R and Leary M (1998) *Resolving Conflicts in Organizations,* Lemos & Crane, London

Activity 8: Making a Plan

Complete the following planning document as you go through a consideration of the approaches discussed in Chapter 6. You will already have details of, for example, whether your case study conflict is hot or cold, and at what level of the Escalator it is at. Now consider the following table of factors and note your thoughts about your first steps towards resolution.

Factor to consider   *Application to living case study*

Factor 1:
Are you prepared?

Factor 2:
How commited
are the parties to
resolution?

Factor 3:
What is the cost
involved?

Factor 4:
Is there an opening
to make a start?

Factor 5:
What is the attitude
of the parties
to the conflict?

Factor 6:
Is the conflict
Hot or Cold?

Factor 7:
At what level is the
conflict and what
is your first approach
to the resolution?

From Fritchie R and Leary M (1998) *Resolving Conflicts in Organizations*,
Lemos & Crane, London

Activity 9: Role Checklist

There are two parts to this Activity. First of all, having read Chapter 7, assess which roles are need in your case study conflict resolution plan. Secondly, consider who will be best placed to carry out the roles. Tick the boxes which are most appropriate to your case study.

Part 1: Which roles are needed?

Moderator	Facilitator	Therapist	Mediator/Arbitrator
☐	☐	☐	☐

Part 2: Who is to carry out the roles?

		Moderator	Facilitator	Therapist	Mediator /Arbitrator
A	Myself as a party in the conflict	☐	☐	☐	☐
B	Another person(s) who is a party in the conflict	☐	☐	☐	☐
C	Myself as a third party (i.e. for a conflict in another area)	☐	☐	☐	☐
D	A third party from another area in the organization	☐	☐	☐	☐

 From Fritchie R and Leary M (1998) *Resolving Conflicts in Organizations*, Lemos & Crane, London

	Moderator	Facilitator	Therapist	Mediator /Arbitrator
E An expert third party from outside the organization	☐	☐	☐	☐
F A third party service which has already been set up	☐	☐	☐	☐

The following table gives examples of the roles which may be most suitable for different levels of conflict

Escalation level	Moderator	Facilitator	Therapist	Mediator /Arbitrator
3 (low level)	A	A		
3 (low level with development opportunities for others sought)	A+B	A+B		
3 (low level in another department)		C		
5 (middle level)		D	D	
6 (middle level)		E	E	E (as mediator)
7–9 (high level)				F (as arbitrator)

Note that these are simplified versions of what might be extremely complex situations, and so your final role decisions may appear much more difficult than the above suggests.

From Fritchie R and Leary M (1998) *Resolving Conflicts in Organizations*, Lemos & Crane, London

Activity 10: Assertiveness Checklist

Especially at low levels of conflict, and particularly in situations where examples of more positive behaviours are needed, assertiveness techniques can be invaluable. Choosing which technique to use in which circumstances needs some thought. As part of the following assertiveness checklist we ask you to think through which situations you are considering when using a particular technique and why you are making that choice. Thinking things through in this way should ensure that you get the best out of the assertiveness techniques you use.

Assertiveness Technique	Where can I see opportunities in my living case study to use this technique	Why have I decided this technique is better than others?
BASIC ASSERTION		
RESPONSIVE ASSERTION		

From Fritchie R and Leary M (1998) *Resolving Conflicts in Organizations*, Lemos & Crane, London

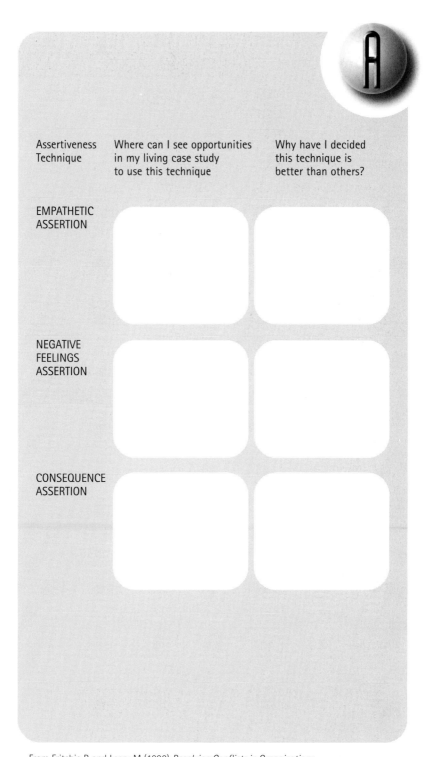

Assertiveness Technique	Where can I see opportunities in my living case study to use this technique	Why have I decided this technique is better than others?
EMPATHETIC ASSERTION		
NEGATIVE FEELINGS ASSERTION		
CONSEQUENCE ASSERTION		

From Fritchie R and Leary M (1998) *Resolving Conflicts in Organizations*, Lemos & Crane, London

Index

180

An invitation to keep in touch

To receive the latest information on forthcoming titles and developments in the Library please return this coupon to our London office at the address below. Also if you would like to comment on our books in any way, we would be happy to hear from you.

--✄

☐ Please include me on the Mike Pedler Library mailing list.

Mr/Ms/Mrs/Miss   First name _____

Surname_____

Position / Organization _____

Department _____

Address_____

_____

_____

Country_____

Postcode _____ Tel _____

Lemos&Crane
20 Pond Square
Highgate Village
London N6 6BA England
Tel: +44 (0)181 348 8263
Fax: +44(0)181 347 5740
E-mail: admin@lemos.demon.co.uk

A Concise Guide to the Learning Organization

Creating and developing learning organizations is an essential quest. But much of the available guidance is criticised for being long-winded and difficult to implement. Now, in *A Concise Guide to the Learning Organization*, **Dr Mike Pedler** and **Kath Aspinwall** show leaders and managers facing unprecedented and unpredictable change how to understand, embrace and harness practical principles, models and approaches that will enhance any organization's capacity to learn. Case examples and "snapshots" of organizations working towards learning are used throughout the book - as are activities that help you evaluate levels of development within your organization.

A Concise Guide to the Learning Organization gives you:
- a practical understanding of the nature of learning and organizational learning, and how the principles of the Eleven Characteristics of the Learning Company can be applied

- an appreciation of the blocks to learning, its limitations, and the shadow side of organizations

- ideas for future development - how learning organizations can contribute to the wider environment, their vital role in the creation of the Good Society.

Dr Mike Pedler, series editor of The Mike Pedler Library, is an adviser to some of Britain's leading companies, Revans Professorial Fellow at the University of Salford, visiting professor at the University of York, co-author of the best-selling *Managing Yourself, A Manager's Guide to Self-development* and *The Learning Company*. His co-author, **Kath Aspinwall**, is a lecturer in education management at Sheffield Hallam University and author (with Mike Pedler) of *Perfect plc?* and *Leading the Learning School*.

ISBN 1-898001-43-X

Also published in the Mike Pedler Library

Dialogue At Work

As much as 75 per cent of a manager's day is spent in conversation. Much practised but imperfectly understood, **Professor Dixon**'s book looks at the nature of talk and how it can be developed to form "dialogue". To manage change, complexity and diversity, organizations and individuals must develop. Individual learning has profound limitations. 'Doing dialogue' or 'development talk' in teams and groups is increasingly being seen as a new essential tool in managing change.

Dialogue At Work gives you:

- an understanding of the relationship between talk and development in organizations, how dialogue differs from the skilled talk that goes on all the time

- skills to recognise talk that hinders learning and development and means of rectifying this on an individual and group basis

- practical ideas to develop forums and conditions for dialogue based on research with leading companies

- summaries of leading theories on the nature and function of dialogue (Argyris, Bohm, Johnson and Johnson, Mezirow, Freire).

Professor Nancy M. Dixon is Associate Professor of Administrative Sciences at The George Washington University, Washington DC. She has served as a consultant to numerous companies including Unisys, Lockheed, General Electric Aircraft Engines, IBM, FAA, Whirlpool, Nippon Telegraph and Telephone Corporation, Japan. She is the acclaimed author of *The Organizational Learning Cycle*.

ISBN 1-898001-41-3

Also published in the Mike Pedler Library

ABC of Action Learning

Professor Reg Revans in this new edition of his classic *ABC of Action Learning* distils the lessons of decades of experience applying the theory he originated - Action Learning - the most important idea to have emerged in management and organizational development since the war. Revans' lifelong mission has been to empower all managers in all organizations to act and to learn from action. The *ABC of Action Learning* sets out practical means of realising his vision. In today's rapidly changing environment where learning is needed to innovate constantly, Revans' ideas are more relevant than ever.

ABC of Action Learning gives you:

- structures to implement action learning programmes based on an understanding of its operational forms

- insights gained from experiences of launching action learning world-wide and responses of top management to efforts to improve their own enterprises

- conditions for bringing about learning in the organization as a whole system.

Professor Reg Revans, creator of action learning, is one of the UK's original business thinkers. A member of the pioneering management team at the National Coal Board after the war, appointed as Britain's first professor of industrial administration in the 1960s, Reg Revans has worked with managers in Britain, Europe, America, Africa and India. He was recently made a Freeman of the City of London.

"interest in Revans' ideas pours in from around the world"
Financial Times

ISBN 1-898001-42-1